How to:
Be More Pirate

Sam Conniff & Alex Barker

First published in the United Kingdom by:
OWN IT! Entertainment Ltd

Company Registration Number: 09154978

Cover design: Chevonne Elbourne

Paperback ISBN: 9781916052345

WWW.OWNIT.LONDON

Contents

PART ONE: Why Pirates?   **1**
Chapter One: Rebellion is the Responsible Choice   3
Chapter Two: Making a Movement   13

PART TWO: Becoming a Pirate   **25**
Chapter Three: The Mutiny Mindset   27
Chapter Four: Live by the Code   44
Chapter Five: Can You Be a Pirate in the Navy?   65

PART THREE: Rewriting the Rules   **79**
Chapter Six: Small Bold Actions   81
Chapter Seven: Go to the Edges of the Map   91
Chapter Eight: Build a Crew   110
Chapter Nine: Re-humanise the System   145
Chapter Ten: Tell a Damn Good Story   170

Chapter Eleven: What Next?   180

The Pirate List 2.0   182
Acknowledgements   187
Biographies   189

PART ONE

Why Pirates?

Chapter One

Rebellion is the Responsible Choice

By Sam Conniff

Rule-breaking, pirates, and real change

At the beginning of *Be More Pirate* there is a dedication to my elder daughter. She was one of the first people to get their hands on a copy and it made her very happy to see her name right in the front. But as she flicked through the pages, she looked puzzled. Which was fair, I thought to myself. Aged five, she didn't read many business books. Thankfully for my ego, it turned out that she wasn't rating me as a sub-par Simon Sinek. She had an even more trenchant criticism. 'Daddy,' she said, looking up at me, 'how did you manage to write a book about pirates with absolutely no pictures in it?' To this day it's the best critique the book has received.

My answer went something like this…

'Well, my love, you see the thing is, your dad thought he'd spent the last 20 years trying to "save the world" until he realised that the well-meant movement of "game changers" was inadvertently often perpetuating problems by allowing identity politics and big ideas like social enterprise to fill the space of "solution finding". This means we didn't ever get to the heart of the matter, which is to say that the problems won't be fixed by fixing the problems, because what's really needed is an overhaul of the engine that's creating the problems. In other words, the business model.

'And perhaps it's time to tell the truth that since the dawn of capitalism, its operating system has been based on exploitation. That

3

was clearest during its foundation perhaps, when people seen as slaves, and sugar, silver, spice, etc. were violently extracted from their natural habitats. Things have got better, but whether you think of it as legacy, DNA or bloodstains, most industries are still shaped by it. So, if we want some kind of capitalism to remain the vehicle for human development, it needs a new engine.

'Hence, pirates as working-class heroes and social revolutionaries: the frustrated millennials of the eighteenth century who decided to rewrite rather than reject society's rules and in so doing laid the foundation of a more sophisticated social contract. That, my darling, is what the book is about, and why there are no pictures.'

That, it turns out, is no way whatsoever to explain the casualty that is capitalism and how to fix it, using pirates as both mechanism and metaphor, to a five-year-old. Depending on your degree of parenting experience or common sense, you may have worked that out for yourself. Sadly, I didn't. I'd let the piratical cat out of the bag and in the following weeks, various bits of bad behaviour were justified with 'I'm breaking the rules, Dad.' I couldn't help but be a bit proud, yet I could see I needed a different way to delineate the crucial difference between good and bad rule-breaking.

My own sanity, not to mention the rocketing blood pressure of my eldest's class teacher, was restored when the perfect learning opportunity presented itself. A few weeks after the book came out, a statue of Millicent Fawcett was unveiled in Parliament Square in London, directly in front of the Houses of Parliament. Millicent was a founder of the Suffragette movement. She led the world in the fight for equal rights for women, and the statue would mark the centenary of women getting the right to vote in the UK. Plus, there has never been a statute of a woman in Parliament Square, ever, and this was the end of a campaign by another pioneering woman, Caroline Criado-Perez, who'd spotted the all-male anachronism and successfully led a people-powered crusade to resolve it. She won the support, raised the funds, and ended up making history. It was just the kind of tale that *Be More Pirate* was celebrating.

So, my daughter and I took the bus to meet Millicent. We talked about the story, helped massively by the fact that the Suffragettes had been a topic at school (which meant the five-year-old knew far more than I did). We discussed the fact that in Millicent's day she wasn't feted for her pioneering and justified rule-breaking so much as castigated for crimes against common decency and the natural order of things. Her reputation, her family, her future, her life, were all in danger. But because she knew she was right, she found the bravery to persevere and helped to shape a change in attitude, culture, and consciousness.

This caught my daughter's imagination, so I tried to tell her the stories behind the other statues in the square.

As anyone who's read *Be More Pirate* can attest, a historian I am not. My retelling left a little to be desired. Churchill? A depressive drunk with a dodgy colonial legacy but a razor-sharp wit and tenacity enough to take the risks that saved us from fascism. Lloyd George: a bristling moustache of a man who both laid the foundations of social insurance and won the First World War while rattling the upper classes by being the last popular Liberal. Gandhi: the pioneer of non-violent protest who helped lead India to independence and whose endlessly quotable wisdom gave a million authors like me a way to start chapters. Etc, etc. ...

Despite my sub-GCSE grasp of history, something became clear to me. We rarely make statues for people who follow orders. In fact, most of our heroes became heroes through an act of rebellion. They could see what was wrong with being 'right' and had the foresight to know that change could come if they could only drag the rest of us over the line.

On the bus home, as we passed along the river, I saw epitaphs for the brave millions who died in numerous wars, which goes to show that we do of course make statues for those who follow orders. Yet in the upper echelons of statue hierarchy, it does seem that breaking the rules is practically a prerequisite. Those 12 leaders in Parliament Square all undoubtedly had their flaws but they were on the right side of history, which is important, a choice, and a choice you need to make.

You might not intend or want to be remembered forever and having a statue made of you a hundred years after you've died is probably not your top priority, but whether you're a leader or a follower, the rules you're using are determining the future. It's your responsibility to look ahead and decide if they're the right ones. Do they deserve you, and do you deserve them? If not, I invite you to dig into this collection of pirate inspiration for the ideas that will fuel your own rebellion.

From cocktails to rebellions

Where did the idea of pirates as unlikely but inspiring role models come from? My daughter may have been baffled by what I was doing (or not doing) with the charming rogues of her picture books, but she wasn't the only one. Plenty of people were unconvinced initially. In our culture, pirates are either a set of clichés for kids' TV shows or a bunch of self-interested career criminals. Credit for any insight about pirates I have come up with must go primarily to the young people I worked with for so many years. I couldn't help but notice their ability to create good trouble, and the agility and effectiveness of their strategies. I began to think of them and refer to them as pirates, in opposition to the establishment navy. So, if the inscription of the book was to my daughter, the deeper dedication was to a different generation of young people: the entrepreneurs, hustlers, and change-makers who were such a big part of my life for nearly 20 years while running Livity. In truth, they were more than that. They were the biggest learning experience of my life and the inspiration for my exploration of what pirates were really all about. I realised that I didn't want to keep on referring to them as 'pirates' without fully knowing what I meant. So eventually I set off on a voyage of discovery that led to *Be More Pirate*.

All the time I was championing them, I was also championing

the incredible and inspiring 'business for good' movement, as well as the social enterprise sector and all its many counterparts – broadly speaking the growing part of the economy wrestling with the balance of trying to do well by doing good.

But something about the way I viewed that world began to change. I have never stopped believing in the value of social business, but I began to suspect that the young people I met were overtaking even the most impressive and established leaders in the sector. And this wasn't true just in the social enterprise space, but in every aspect of life, from technology to education, from politics to business. I saw less and less inspiration from traditional modes of leadership and many more examples of leadership coming from the next generation. A pivot was taking place, where instead of looking up for role models, young people were increasingly looking sideways at one another for new ways to navigate unknown waters. I began to appreciate that the last thing my cohorts of young pirates should do was look up to their leaders, who were largely the self-interested people who'd got us all into such a mess in the first place.

It was around this time that I attended a cocktails and canapés world-saving shindig where the benchmark for being out of touch reached new lows. In the break before I was due to do my thing, I nipped to the loos. Out in the conference, brands and businesses earnestly debated helping those who were suffering. But in the loo, we had temperature controls that adjusted the toilets seat to make them the perfect warmth for our arse cheeks. When helping 'poor people' happens from bottom-warming bathrooms, it's time to start the fucking revolution.

As I've said, I still believe that converting the catalyst of capitalism can reduce its harmful emissions. I'm proud of my contribution to the social enterprise movement which I think is driven by sincere intention, smart people, and brands beginning to realise that meaning means more than marketing. But... intentions ain't actions, and therein lies the mother-fucking-rub come judgement day. It's what we do that counts, not what we argue, believe or think. And so, as I warmed my cosy bum on the perfect 23-degree smugness of conscious capitalism, about to be the twentieth white man to address the room, I wrote a new speech. 'With respect, I call bullshit on us, me included. Us the well-off, well-intended, and well, let's face it, similar-looking and sounding attendees of today's event. The future world we want to save won't look like us. It's young, brown, global, innovative and uninvited.' Or words to that effect. I meant it with love and respect, but I hope it felt like love and respect wrapped around a brick.

I had to start breaking my own rules again. It wasn't long after the heated loo-seat speech that I faced up to the fact that I, for one, needed some different leaders to look up to. The Livity pirates did, too. That's when I embraced Golden Age Pirates as the missing role models of the hour and decided to overcome my dyslexia, and the chip on my shoulder about not going to university, and write a book called *Be More Pirate, or How To Take On the World and Win*. To my delight the book was a bestseller, but much more amazingly, thousands of you took it to heart and began rising up in rebellion. At first, I didn't believe it, but soon I found myself staring down the barrel of a difficult decision. And then I learned to be careful what I wished for.

I had wished for people-powered radical change that moves fast and far in the direction of a better world. I had wished for a more optimistic outlook for my children to inherit as they grow up. I had wished for change that doesn't come with a brand message for some shit we don't need or a membership that most of us can't afford. And now here it was, and it scared me.

I received thousands of messages from organisations, individuals, private businesses, public policy, finance, tech, start-ups, and more... across every sector, industry, age, seniority, and job title. In all of them there was a dawning admission that permission-based change, where good ideas are sent to die in PowerPoint slides and email threads, can't match the demand of disruption knocking down the door.

At first, I struggled to find the confidence to live up to this response. I shared my doubts about whether I was ready or right to try to make this a movement and was supportively told to 'Man the fuck up and rise to the occasion.' But still I didn't mobilise the moment. I would run as fast as I could to keep up with my new life as an author, then race home every day to see my young daughters, always caught in the same paradox. 'Sorry kids, I'm so worried about your future but I can only half-bake the rebellion right now,' vs 'Sorry rebellion, I know you're gathering momentum but it's bath time, then I need to read *The Gruffalo* five times, before raising some invoices and writing something funny on Instagram to hustle up a few speaking gigs.'

But quite rightly, the new pirates didn't care about any of that. They just wanted to get started. When I received the message below I realised that I had to do something, but I didn't have to do it all on my own. (And yes, I know, it's quite the irony that I wrote a book about gathering a crew around you to create change and still struggled to welcome them on board and hand over to them when they actually turned up.)

Dear Sam, I finished Be More Pirate – thank you – it's brilliant, just what's needed! I'm officially ready for my first rebellion so here goes... I signed up to join the community, excited to be inspired and meet potential crew members but then realised I was just signing up to a newsletter :(Pirates would draw strength from each other – hearing each other and rebelling together. So I have a proposal – I will start a community of pirates offline meet-ups, first in London. Let me know if you would join us or even play a part in making it happen?'

Gulp. Well, yes, obviously, and please to both! We spoke, we met, and the crew began to form. Then there was another reader, and another rebellion... An investor with a sense of ethics called Chris Kingsman gave me the money to employ the support I needed for six months as we got a community established. I embraced my good fortune and set out to find the perfect Right Hand Pirate. And I did.

This is how I advertised it:

Right Hand Pirate wanted for adventures in Good Trouble. A 12-month contract to help me harness the community that's sprung up behind my book (@BeMorePirate) into a meaningful movement of positive change.

Mostly Community Manager, Partly PA, all Pirate. Please take a look, share or tag anyone with the right experience, sense of adventure and ambition to change the world. Pirate-style.

There were a few key elements to the job description and brief that I sent to the hundreds of people who applied. The first was a question. How do we use this moment and momentum to change the world and make Be More Pirate go global? The second was more of a plea. Can you help me balance 1) Getting out of debt, 2) Not compromising my ambition for social impact, and 3) Making a new career out of this while, 4) Stopping me from disappearing up my own arse? That was pretty much it. Working hours would be set by them, as long as a) We got shit done and b) We connected meaningfully once a week.

I narrowed it down to a shortlist, all of whom were incredible, but only one really took me to task and pointed out the misstep I'd made by following exactly in the footsteps of the world-saving mob I'd previously called out. She made it clear that 'going global', or anything else that made scale the measure of success, was the antithesis of my own argument. If the only outcome that mattered was meaningful change, then it would be better to focus on doing one thing well than worry about egocentric metrics like the size of the community.

Not only did Alex get the job, she also made me move the date of the prematurely assembled first meet-up, which allowed it to become the genesis of the movement that came next.

There was rarely a week where she didn't live and breathe each part of the role, especially as I began to learn to be a public speaker and be treated like 'talent', which felt impactful and exciting and was also a bigger opportunity for disappearing up my own arse than even I'd anticipated. But that wasn't the biggest distraction. A lot of personal turbulence played out that year, the likes of which I'd never known. I would never have been able to keep the ship afloat alone. Alex stepped in to deliver events when I suddenly couldn't make them, and supportively but strongly stopped me from cutting corners when I found it hard to focus.

We developed our own Pirate Code and travelled up and down the UK on trains to Wales, Manchester, Newcastle, and wherever communities of pirates were gathering. We met a new generation of pirates, who changed our outlook on what is to come next. Rightly, this book is about them, and, rightly, it's been mainly curated and written by Alex.

At the end of the year, we decided that Alex would take over from me, no longer Right Hand Pirate but full pirate in her own right. We made our plans for Alex to take charge just as Covid-19 hit, lockdown began, and this book was due to go to print. Instinctively, the controlling part in me wanted to press pause and stay in charge. As my other projects dissolved, this part panicked.

But, by the time you read this Alex will have been named Captain, Pirate Queen or whatever she chooses to call herself for some while, leading the community with the courage, conviction, critical thinking, and occasional self-doubt that made her the perfect pirate for both jobs. And now, if, as we've been hearing from people, the message of *Be More Pirate* has even greater relevance in a crisis (and there are sure to be more crises to come), then the last thing we need is for power to be retained in classic forms, i.e. by white men of privilege thinking they know best.

And if the story of what happened after *Be More Pirate* was published has taught me anything, it's that I didn't understand the importance and power of the principles I'd tapped into. I had no idea how effective the original pirates' techniques would be when taken forward by the pirates-in-waiting the book found. I didn't even grasp how they would transform my own life. Becoming a pirate in my forties did way more for me and those I love than the laboured attempt at growing up that was my thirties. At a time when I was trying to discover how to reconcile responsibility and freedom, and the waters of my life were very stormy indeed, the metaphor of pirates allowed me to face my fears and sail past them to a place of real freedom. And no matter where you are on the long arc of realising who you're meant to be, I am sure pirates can help you, too. The proof is within these pages.

We are living through times when sharing power is more important than ever. We all have a duty to protect the importance of freedom, both individual and collective. When I began to write *Be More Pirate*, I felt the world was slipping into crisis, and I was convinced that we all hold the answers. As we evolve out of and into new forms of crisis, I grow more convinced that only a rebellion will do, that we need new, fairer rules to live and work by, and that we must all write them together. Be More Pirate is no longer my idea, if it ever was. It's not even mine and Alex's idea. It's our idea. It's all the stories of the real-life pirates bringing it to life, whose patterns, tactics, and pirate tricks you're about to learn. It's your idea, if you embrace it and I hope you will. After nearly three years of pirate voyaging, I feel that the essence of pirate is one part freedom and the fight never to lose it, one part power and how we must share it, and a third part connection. Because none of this matters without each other.

Sam
sam@samconniff.com

Chapter Two

Making a Movement

By Alex Barker

All aboard

For me, the adventure began on a freakishly warm day in February 2019. I was sitting in a pub on the South Bank of the River Thames, trying to appreciate the moment I had arrived at. Despite my father's protective warnings that this was a job like any other and I should treat it as such, I didn't really believe him. I was overcome with the feeling that what I *thought* I'd signed up for, was probably not what I'd *actually* signed up for. Right Hand Pirate didn't sound like a job. It sounded like a mission.

I was also privately thanking the weather gods for not pissing down on our pirate parade. In two hours' time, 100 or so people were due to descend onto the *Golden Hinde*, the rather incongruous replica of Francis Drake's ship that's moored by London Bridge. If everyone who was invited turned up, I was not sure whether the creaking, cramped boat would be able to house them.

In truth, I was very nervous. I had never met any of these people before, only emailed them blindly. In one way or another, they had all responded to the book, and now I had a folder bulging with over 500 detailed messages; stories that over the next year would make me laugh and cry in equal measure. But back then I just really hoped I wouldn't let them down.

In an attempt to be organised, I'd sent Sam some briefing notes ahead of time, including a list of all the people who'd volunteered to stand up and speak at the event. I wanted to spend this final hour running over it to make sure we knew who everyone was. I was used to doing things by the book – it was the only way I'd ever been taught to do anything. When Sam arrived, I enquired as to whether he'd read over the notes, but he just looked at me with a half apologetic smile.

We had a chat and a pint instead.

An hour later, lo and behold, those 100 people did show up, and most of my concerns about the difficulties of moving around on a sixteenth-century ship were realised. They simply couldn't. The smattering of tall men stayed wedged into spots where their heads could fit between the low beams. This, plus the strategic placement of barrels, created a tedious low-level obstacle course. So, speed networking was out.

But it didn't matter in the slightest – everyone was whooping and cheering and slopping their booze about the deck. We opened up the middle level (the gun deck) so that people could sit and look down into the bottom where the speakers were positioned to pitch to the audience. I'd allotted 10 people just two minutes each to announce a rebellion that they wanted to start or join, which of course rapidly escalated into however long they fancied.

In the middle of the chaos, I realised there was something special about this gathering. I'd spent the last nine years working for charities and had been involved in countless networking events designed to bring people together to talk about ideas for positive social change, or something along those lines. This felt very different to any of those events. Looking around, you'd be hard pressed to understand why all these people were meeting. There was no single issue or sector to bind them. No membership to a club. The group was inclusive of age, gender, class, and race.

But more than that, the energy was different. It wasn't quite a party, but nor was it strictly professional. People were riled up, but not angry. Beneath the obvious frustration with the Brexit stalemate, social inequalities, and the inevitability of climate change, there was a gleeful anticipation. Of what, I didn't yet know.

Finding method in the madness

This book traces one year of our movement and outlines a vision for change. It is not an academic analysis or a complete theory, instead we have deliberately rooted all our evidence and conviction in real people's lives and testimonies: their moments of bravery and revelation, their missteps and mischief.

We decided to start from this place because it is not the done thing. Every year hundreds of books are published filled with frameworks and theories for change yet rarely are they grounded in the messiness of people's lives. There is an enormous void between the streams of research, policies and shiny examples of technological innovation coming out of government, think tanks and academia, and the limited capacity that we have as citizens to engage, or put them into practice.

It is, therefore, unsurprising that politics fails to speak to people, fails to represent them, and fails to deliver solutions that work, because we are starting from the wrong place. This is not to say there is no value in theory, or in new ideas, but we have to do the dirty work of implementation and deal more honestly with everything that gets in the way, day to day: the procrastination and frustration, power dynamics and peer pressure. Fear and admin.

This was part of the status quo I wanted to disrupt when I came to work with Sam and move *Be More Pirate* towards a movement. I wanted to close this gap between theoretical ideas about change, and what is really going on. With that in mind, part of my job has always been to interrogate Sam's own framework – the alluring, alliterative 5Rs in *Be More Pirate* – and see how much bearing it had on reality:

1. Rebel – draw strength by standing up to the status quo
2. Rewrite – bend, break, but most importantly rewrite the rules

3. Reorganise – collaborate to achieve scale, rather than growth
4. Redistribute – fight for fairness, share power, and make an enemy of exploitation
5. Retell – weaponise your story, then tell the hell out of it

5 Rs. Feels too convenient to me.

Hence one of the first questions I asked Sam in my interview was, 'Do you think *Be More Pirate* is more style over substance?' It felt a bit impertinent, but I also felt like I had nothing to lose. I was looking for something different, something without any of the usual bullshit, and if this wasn't it, I was happy to walk away.

Institution to revolution

My own story echoes many of those you'll read in this book because I found *Be More Pirate* while I was at a crossroads in my life. By 'found' I mean I downloaded the first chapter on my Kindle, along with 40 other sample first chapters (tell-tale sign of a crossroads-but-could-be-a-crisis). I read the first few pages of Sam's book and immediately put it down. I had absolutely no appetite to read a book about social change. I'd had enough of that.

For the previous seven years I'd worked at the RSA (long title: Royal Society for the Encouragement for the Arts, Manufactures, and Commerce), as a communications manager for their membership department. The RSA is a 260-year-old society-turned-social innovation charity and think tank, bearing the tagline 'twenty-first-century enlightenment'. Indeed, it was born out of the enlightenment era; the RSA had humble(ish) beginnings in a Covent Garden coffee shop, the vision of 11 men wanting to do 'undertakings for the publick good.'

While I was researching some additional pirate history for this book, I heard that phrase again, in a line spoken by Nathaniel North when he was elected a pirate captain. He pledged a 'commitment to "doing every Thing which may conduce to the publick Good".[1] It was only then that it dawned on me how soon after the end of piracy the RSA was founded, and how they were both a response to social injustice.

The RSA was radical in the beginning. They were the first membership organisation of the era to admit women. They offered prizes for inventions that would improve the lives of ordinary people. In 1802 they offered a premium for mechanical means of cleaning chimneys,[2] which helped to abolish the employment of children doing that particular kind of dirty work. They challenged what was deemed acceptable.

But I left in 2018, because I had come to believe that much of the social innovation sector had drifted very far from what it professed to stand for. Rather than change the status quo, it seemed to entrench it. Power was concentrated rather than distributed. Everything was done in a certain way and only certain people were listened to. It had become an echo chamber to the nth degree. The impact of all this, over time, was unsettling. I was seeing too many colleagues and friends with their self-esteem in tatters because they felt silenced, undervalued, and fundamentally unable to change anything. I'm not sure I'd be brave enough to raise this publicly if it were just one or two people, but when you can name dozens with similar complaints, it would be wrong to turn a blind eye.

Dissent, however, is buried beneath a mass of liberal sounding reports that make you question over and over whether you've gotten it wrong. How could this be possible here? I'm not sure there is anything more disheartening and bewildering than the moment when the veil is lifted and you realise your heroes might be villains, and that you no longer have a compass to understand what's good in the world.

1   p.30 The Invisible Hook, Leeson, Peter, T.

2   www.thersa.org/fellowship/fellowship-news/fellowship-news/rsa-history-premiums-for-chimney-brushes

For a long time I accepted that 'this is how it is', and there are limits to what can be changed. That is utter nonsense of course; there are examples everywhere to disprove it, but when you are surrounded by that story, it becomes true. The bigger question I had to ask myself was: am I willing to speak out, or do anything? When I looked starkly back at the history, when some became pirates, and others formed new institutions, I could see a fork in my own path. It felt like history was simply repeating itself; it's still a fight to redistribute power and improve people's working conditions. We're still not there with equal pay, or equal say or a system that looks after marginalised groups.

So this time, I choose pirates.

The crew that took on the Home Office

Thankfully, I discovered, through the many conversations I had in order to gather the stories in this book, that there is a great deal of both substance and impact to *Be More Pirate*. For all the Rs, and the bright pink 'Pirates fuck shit up' slogans we throw into presentations, behind it is a truly authentic voice. Over the year my belief in Sam has only strengthened by seeing him continually return to what he believes in and act on it, as well as putting a hell of a lot of faith in me when there were no guarantees. I am forever grateful to him for being a real leader, not just for me, but for everyone in this book.

But, certainly, the greatest thing about *Be More Pirate* is how it has mobilised people to act.

One of those people was a young woman called Natalie Clarkson. When a preview copy of the book landed on her desk in 2018, she had no idea quite how valuable it would prove to be. Natalie already had a fight on her hands. She and a few others were in the midst of campaigning to have their friend Opelo Kgari released from Yarl's Wood Immigration Removal Centre where she had been detained for three months, facing deportation.

Opelo came with her mother to the UK from Botswana at

the age of 13 – legally. It wasn't until she was 18 and applying to universities that she discovered that her immigration status was not as straightforward as she thought. Opelo's immigration story is striking because it began five years after she arrived and did not conclude for a further 10 years. Ten years in limbo, unable to further her education, or make many major life decisions that require full citizenship.

During this period Opelo and her mother were moved by the authorities from their home in Birmingham to Stoke-on-Trent, which was where she and Natalie first met through a local church group. In January 2018, things started to escalate, and not in the direction they hoped. Following a short stint the previous year at Yarl's Wood, Opelo was required to check in with the local immigration office in Stoke-on-Trent every two weeks. One day, upon going to her regular appointment, she was guided outside to a van and taken back to Yarl's Wood. She remained there for three months, during which time a small group of friends, including Natalie, began to rally around her case, starting with a few supportive acts to make Opelo's life more bearable:

'We'd take her clothes and deposit money in her account for the shop, that sort of thing.'

But then things got really serious.

'I remember, it was a Saturday afternoon. I was out shopping when Opelo called me and said they'd put her in a van and were taking her to the airport. She was going to be deported. She said she'd literally scribbled down three numbers and mine was one but had no idea what to do.'

Natalie and her crew quickly assembled a plan; a couple of them drove to the airport, while another contacted their local MP who already knew about Opelo's case, and in this instance managed to succeed in stopping the deportation.

'I'm not quite sure how she did it but this really kicked us into gear and I realised we needed to do something. They were serious about deporting her. I was reading Be More Pirate *at the time and it was at the question – what was I willing to fight for? – that I began to think,*

maybe we could do this. But it was the bits about organising as a crew that made me rethink how. I realised we needed to be more strategic, organised, and wait for the right moment to strike.'

As a result, everyone started to take on specific roles, they set up a Facebook group and organised a proper campaign. Then came a petition on Change.Org which gained 2,000 signatures within three days. A journalist friend advised that the Home Office dislikes media attention so any noise in the press would help the case. Natalie utilised her press contacts and spoke on the *Victoria Derbyshire Show*, as well as local radio in Stoke, and they managed to gain significant coverage of the case in *The Independent*. Besides their local MP, a few others began to speak out and Opelo and her mother even got a mention in parliament.

Just when the noise was starting to really ramp up, another attempt was made to deport Opelo.

This time, her lawyers stepped in to prevent it, she was returned to Yarl's Wood then very quickly given a court date for November 2018 and sent back home. The lawyers told Natalie that at this stage, the only real chance to prevent her deportation was to stay in the media and kick up a fuss. So, they doubled down, gained more signatures on the petition, Natalie went back on television and tried to keep the pressure up.

Then they hit another hurdle. Not long after she returned home, Opelo's lawyer changed and the replacement wasn't happy with all the media exposure the case was getting. Natalie and crew had to suddenly stop everything, sit tight, and hope they'd done enough.

Finally, a week before the court case was due to go ahead, Opelo phoned Natalie and told her it wasn't happening. It wasn't postponed; it was cancelled altogether.

She'd been given temporary leave to remain for two and a half years.

'I was in the office when she called, and I just burst in tears. I couldn't really believe it.

I am clearly more of a pirate than I thought.'

This must be the place

Natalie's story speaks to the reality of what *Be More Pirate* is, as a movement. I often refer to people in the network, as 'the crew' but really it is like a fleet of ships, a coming together of strong-minded captains, many leading crews of their own. Each person has interpreted the ideas in their own way and is fighting their own corner. I wanted to properly understand and value the work they were doing, instead of simply 'proving success' by doubling a newsletter list. What was the point in a crew if at the end I didn't really know anyone?

Six and a half months after the *Golden Hinde* event, we decided to hold another big gathering. Having achieved peak pirate with an actual ship, I had in my mind a very clear picture of the kind of place I wanted to hold it this time around. Somewhere that felt a bit renegade and underground, but still had community spirit. I trekked around a few venues, but came up against barriers of cost, or availability. Sam only had one possible day free in September, so I had no room to manoeuvre. Precariously close to the deadline, I visited a warehouse in Bermondsey that is home to art students, martial arts, and meditation groups. It honestly looked like a 1980s car park – the lifts had long since been abandoned due to the asbestos hazard. It was one of those places you'd never, ever find by chance.

After puffing up the four flights of stairs, I found the building manager Toby, who took me to the space advertised.

Upon entering, my heart sunk. It was grey, cold, bare, and far, far too big to decorate, realistically. I was just about to leave, deflated and with no more ideas left on the list, when Toby suggested looking at one other space at the back.

As soon as I walked in, I knew, like that old Talking Heads song – *This Must be the Place*. On the wall was a giant piece of graffiti: L.O.V. E but instead of the O, a skull.

*

We held the event on the same day as one of the big youth climate strikes. I'd advertised it as a late summer party, because I'd imagined replicating the riotous fun on the *Golden Hinde*, until I realised I'd fallen into my own trap again. I thought there was a formula but *Be More Pirate* doesn't replicate. It's always stepping into the unknown, never a recipe, always the testing ground.

The deep uncertainty over Brexit (still), and the inertia around the climate crisis despite Extinction Rebellion's momentous efforts to shake people out of complacency, was beginning to feel like a weight on everyone's shoulders. The seven speakers took a more serious tone this time, and I was beginning to grasp the full extent of what making a movement is really about.

The line that has always stood out to me in *Be More Pirate* was: *We need to become more comfortable with being uncomfortable.* It had always felt to me like the missing ingredient in all the change initiatives I'd been part of. We were talking about the 'right' subjects but with a particular kind of language that sidestepped anything too inconvenient, tricky or taboo. In doing so we did everyone a huge disservice. I knew that it was time to invite some of this in, so I opened the event by asking everyone to network by telling others something they wouldn't usually share – a memory they regret, or the last time they cried. Something that is difficult to talk about. Vulnerability leads to trust, and you simply can't build a strong network without that.

In the days after, we received messages from people saying that it was a moving and memorable night; that they'd felt real solidarity and had conversations with people they'd never normally encounter. But the thing that stayed with me most, was the woman who'd said she'd experienced goosebumps. This, I realised, was what I had been craving at all the events I used to attend. *Of course.* Change begins with getting people to feel something.

I can't honestly give any better advice other than to abandon the plan, and lead from the heart.

From then on, I began thinking of movement building very differently. I understood that the chemistry between people in the room was more important than the numbers or putting on a big old fanfare. It was the kind of chemistry I'd found over and over with the people I'd sat down with to interview for this book, when you know you're looking at a true ally. Writing this during the weird months of coronavirus, it was talking to the crew that made lockdown bearable and even inspiring. I am very lucky that so many of them I now consider friends.

That evening was a demonstration of what this whole book is about. We are persuaded, convinced, and moved to act, because of each other. I heard over and over, that more people would take up arms when they could see others doing it so this book grew in size. However, it was impossible to capture everyone's ideas and stories; those who do feature are simply individuals we were able to get to know in more depth, or who have taken their ideas further. There are many, many more to come, I'm sure.

*

'When individuals participate in a social movement, even if it doesn't achieve anything, it is usually a transformative experience.'

I heard this quote at an event; it's stayed with me since, as it neatly sums up why Sam and I have both become frustrated with endless talk about change and not enough action. Doing *something*, anything really, can be the unexpected catalyst for inner change. Even if what you do is unsuccessful. Doing stuff gets you out of ruts and leads you to people and places that you could never possibly have imagined otherwise. But you have to start.

The pages that follow are a dedication to every single person who has stepped up, stepped out of line, and tried to set a new precedent. The system as a whole might feel impenetrable but it stacks up to what we each choose to do or not to do every day. The hand on every lever not yet pulled is probably shaking, yet this is the *real* work. The hard stuff, but it is also the tonic and the truth that we need.

PART TWO

Becoming a Pirate

Chapter Three

The Mutiny Mindset

*I'm sure you can imagine the fear, frustration, and anger
I felt. But there was something else forming underneath
all of that, something new. It was resolve.*

Julie Reid

Pirates = permission

The journey to becoming a pirate begins with discontent. It
starts from a place of dissatisfaction with the established order, a
nagging feeling that there must be a better way to do things; that
there must be more to work, life, *existence* than this, whatever 'this'
happens to be for you.

You might have a sense that your day-to-day work is irrelevant
compared with the bigger picture. Maybe you're exhausted by the
expectation that you will work into the evening, every evening, for
no extra pay, and your health, relationships, and family are cracking
under the weight. You might be discontented with the lack of
affordable childcare where you live, or seriously unimpressed with
the unoriginal thinking coming from your boss, your teacher, or
your country's leaders.

Or maybe you simply can't shake the feeling that real life is
happening somewhere else.

If you can see a storm or two brewing on the horizon, and you'd
appreciate some suggestions from others who've already set their
own course, then stay with us. *Be More Pirate* reframed the most

notorious pirates in history as innovators and social revolutionaries, but with this book Sam and I want to take it much further. The people within these pages are evidence that role-playing pirate is a fast track route to courage, conviction, and getting shit done. So, I will not short-change the ambition: I want to change the cultural definition of 'pirate' for good.

In the 1600s (or thereabouts), there was a saying: *Those who would go to sea for pleasure, would go to hell as a pastime.*[3] Being a sailor in the navy, or on a merchant ship, was an utterly wretched existence. Conditions were so grim that around 40% of the crew died on any voyage. Unsurprisingly, almost no one signed up voluntarily so press gangs were sent around London and other ports to hunt down men and force them on board. All kinds of underhand tactics were used to harangue people into this line of work.

Now consider why someone might turn to piracy. Popular culture has long had us believing that people became pirates because they were inherently greedy, had a bigger appetite for violence, and a flagrant disregard for the law. Only the latter is really true, and rightly so when the laws of supposedly civilised nations regarded human life so little. Pirates simply stopped partaking in an unfair system. For selfish reasons yes, but by refusing the system, they created a new one by default.

Becoming a pirate was first and foremost about giving yourself permission to no longer be miserable.

What would it mean then, if we viewed our discontent not as a personal failing or a pathology, but as a rational response and as the necessary impetus to create something radically better? How would things be different if we viewed our dissatisfaction not as weakness – something to dismiss, hide or bury – but simply as a message? A signal on the horizon trying to redirect you. Because in the midst of our discomfort sometimes another more powerful voice emerges, and it says 'enough'.

3   P.36 The Republic of Pirates, Woodward, Colin,

Pirates vs rebels

In every *Be More Pirate* workshop I've ever run, there's nearly always one voice that pipes up with something along these lines: *I'm the pirate! I've never taken things at face value; I've always disrupted and been the rebel in the group.*

The sentiment would leave me feeling puzzled. Given everything I'd learned about piracy something about this didn't ring true. I've since realised it's because it reflects the tired misconception that pirates are archetypal rebels – agents of chaos armed with a 'rules are there to be broken' attitude. This of course is not true, and it's worth understanding the distinction.

Pirates, as we know, were originally sailors in the navy, ordinary people who learned and tried to play by the rules. It is therefore impossible to have *always* been a pirate because the process of 'becoming' is essential. Their experience of the system was what gave pirates motivation, and understanding its flaws enabled them to create something better. So even if you have always felt that inner burning of frustration (and so always felt like a pirate in disguise), it's the moment of making a decision, of moving from insider to outsider, that is so crucial.

Being *more* pirate is an ongoing repositioning of yourself in relation to the rules. A pirate is not a fixed personality type, or an archetype of any kind, because it is not a permanent state: if it were, it would become predictable and would lose what is so essential about it in the first place. If you always do one particular thing because you think it is 'pirate', you have missed the point. The pirate rebellion is a creative one, a continual reinvention, so it cannot be any one activity – there is never recourse to automatically *attack* or do whatever worked last time. It's a way of *being* that is continually disrupting itself. This fluidity enables a more sophisticated response to changing circumstances, and it's what makes pirates unpredictable and powerful.

And this is where I strike the first cross through Sam's 5R framework. Right through Rebel, because I don't believe it is step one. Rebellion – standing up to the status quo – is hard. If it wasn't, we'd all be doing it. Instead, there are a multitude of forces pushing us in the opposite direction towards conformity and safety. What I learned fairly quickly from our community was that in order to rebel and begin challenging something in the outside world, you first have to undergo an inner rebellion – that moment of giving yourself permission. **To stand up to the status quo, first you have to stand up to yourself.** You have to decide to reject the feeling of limitation and powerlessness within. This is step one.

This chapter explores the alchemy of that internal shift: what we might call the mutiny mindset.

Finding power in a crisis

'Perhaps it was growing up in a religious family. Or perhaps it was that my father was in the military. Both are institutions with a long list of rules and punishments for stepping out of line. Whatever the reason, I've always been a girl who played by the rules and tried to be obedient. I found comfort in following orders.'

Ohio-born Julie Reid had always wanted to be a writer. After graduating from college, she dreamed of moving to New York, eager to dip her toes in the water of freelance writing but quickly found that she lacked the confidence.

'I'm an introvert and the thought of going up to people and interviewing them was too much. I was so paralysed by the fear of being laughed at.'

Writing is largely an exercise in vulnerability – it's difficult to write well without sharing something of yourself. And, it requires an ability to voice new, unconventional or even unwelcome ideas; it compels you to be a leader, not a follower, and that is difficult when you're used to the opposite. So instead Julie took a more practical route and got herself a job in digital marketing, which felt like the next best thing. Until it wasn't. As she progressed up the ladder she watched her salary and happiness diverge. Despite the feeling deep down that the role was entirely incompatible with her character and her interests she became an account manager.

The financial stability that came with the title meant that life cantered on, as it does. Julie moved to England for a fresh start, and in 2012, got married, settling for a while in London before moving to a town near Leeds where she took up another unexciting, but familiar, well-paid agency role. Mercifully, a year or so into the job an unexpected door opened, and she was given the opportunity to head up a new department leading on content design and strategy. Here was the chance to pivot her career back in a more creative direction and finally find her own voice.

Just as things had gotten underway, the winds changed, again.

'I started reading Be More Pirate *right before my company announced redundancies due to financial strains. They sat me down and told me that I was being put on notice and it was likely I would be let go within two weeks.'*

Her performance wasn't the issue, she had done well in appraisals, and was hitting the revenue targets. But her new department wasn't yet bringing in enough business for the company to continue to float it with their current finances. Not only that, the whole situation was being badly handled. There was little transparency, communication was poor, and Julie received sparse support from the senior team. When she hit that two-week warning mark, they extended her notice by another two weeks, and instructed her to fill her pipeline with incoming work to try to save herself.

'I'm sure you can imagine the fear, frustration, and anger I felt. But there was something else forming underneath all of that, something new.

'It was resolve.

'Ten years into my career, I could look back over the jobs I'd had and see a pattern emerging. I'd always taken jobs out of fear. The need for stability or a certain salary led me further down a route I didn't even want to be on. Many of the companies I'd worked for were ego-driven and financially motivated. Employee churn was high with

people burning out regularly. I'd only just started to picture what type of future I wanted for myself, but I lacked confidence to give it a try.'

This is when the book (rather ironically handed to her by her boss), gave Julie the courage she needed. Specifically, these few lines:

No one is coming to save you. It's going to get worse before it gets better. There's an urgency in the air and a need for change. Today, if we want to improve this picture, of our future, we have to do it ourselves.

'This hit me hard. I finished Be More Pirate *and immediately started it again. I did the exercises at the end of each chapter and spent hours clarifying what I wanted my life to be about. I knew that now was the time to take a chance on myself.'*

Julie began looking around for other opportunities and soon found a role with a start-up that she would previously have never dared apply for. It was a small company aligned with a cause she believed in, where she would be able to write and create interesting content. Then, in an odd twist of fate, at the end of the second two weeks of her notice period, she was told that it was being revoked. Some additional work had come through and everything could go back to the way it was – 'as if this little blip hadn't happened'.

'The only problem was that I wasn't the same. I had turned pirate.'

Piracy 101: listen to yourself

So Julie had a clear choice. She could stay and stick it out with a company who didn't really value her, or she could leave with no guarantee that she would land the other role.

Of course, this newly turned pirate jumped ship.

Within weeks she'd interviewed successfully at the start-up, and still works for them today. She's now head of content so ostensibly can shape everything on the site and is using it to start asking more provocative questions about what twenty-first-century global citizenship looks like.

The point, however, is this: Julie's hand was forced by what at first appeared to be a crisis, only she discovered that turbulence can in fact be a gift – the beginning of real agency. This is not a flippant comment intended to trivialise suffering or difficulty, but a truth often acknowledged by those who have experienced adversity, and one we would be remiss to ignore. The crumbling of the castle walls only reveals how fragile and limited this external security was to begin with. Julie had spent most of her life playing it safe and shielding herself from unemployment, but when it happened, it was the beginning of something far better. **In always protecting ourselves against endings we also prevent beginnings.**

Confronted with her company's poor finances and the loss of her job, Julie didn't collapse but instead sprang into action. The realisation that no one is coming to save you is a profound one, simultaneously gutting and deeply liberating. The irony of course is that to truly know it, you have to have first believed that the answers do lie elsewhere, and that someone or something else will save the day.

At the end of chapter four in *Be More Pirate* the question is asked: *When did you first stand up to power?* It's there to remind you of your own source of power – what gets you fired up and how it feels. If we do not know the source of power in ourselves, we easily and unconsciously give it away, or make the assumption that it exists elsewhere – in authority, money or status. Too often they become false gods. They are the people or places that say no, make you feel small or afraid, and in doing that, they steal the power that is inherently yours.

So this is the real first step to becoming pirate – when you no longer look outwards in order to understand what to do, but look to yourself and ask what really matters. The absence of external stability gives you nowhere else to turn, other than to yourself.

Throw a better party

In 2017, Jim Edmondson found himself in a similar position to Julie; he had a choice to make. For the last 10 years he had run a highly successful tech company that sold cutting edge engineering solutions all over the world. He had grown the team from just two to 90 UK employees, and by the end of that year raised upwards of $70 million, with offices in China and the US. Jim was a *really* good salesman, but personally he was lost.

'It was one of those turning points where my marriage fell apart, I was really down, and I didn't know which direction to go in. I'd been on this crack cocaine salary trail, following someone else's vision for so long... So, after 10 years, with a huge stake in the company, I just left.'

Not knowing quite what it was he was looking for, Jim began dabbling in consultancy – teaching other businesses about leadership and profit generation. Yet the fulfilment he'd found in his early career, the innovation and the problem solving, was gone. Nothing was sticking. It was his then girlfriend who gave him a copy of *Be More Pirate* to read one day while they were on holiday.

'At first I thought, I really don't want to read someone else's business book, but I didn't have much else to do. I got into a hammock and started reading and it was like a lightbulb came on. Everything just connected. Boom.'

Growing up in Bermuda, Jim had always surfed and like many of us had become increasingly concerned about the impact of ocean waste, but couldn't quite get on board with becoming an eco-warrior. So much of the environmental narrative touted by NGOs and activists ran counter to his understanding of capitalism as a means to a better quality of life; he didn't know how to fit into the story.

But, sitting in a hammock surrounded by the ocean, his mind filled with the image of pirates battling the waves, it suddenly became clear that his purpose was not to try to fit in with what already existed. He could create something entirely different. The idea that came forth was to build a new type of investment fund that would *only* invest in green technologies – a skull and crossbones of finance.

'We've all known for a long time we're fucking up the environment, we know we need to change but most of us don't want to. We only really

innovate in crises, but the best innovations come from free market scenarios instead of soft money from charity. So, there has to be both an urgent need and the free market to force it to be a business. I thought, here is a way to really shake up the finance industry. If the pirates could do this 300 years ago, then surely so could we.'

Jim returned home to figure out his plan and within months, TAKK Cap was born: a fund that would invest in lean but growing companies that focus on environmental innovations, with a preference for those that also have a strong people-first culture. The idea behind the fund was to show that you can use market forces to speed up the development of new technologies that will reduce global warming *and* generate decent profit. Jim firmly believed there was a clear opportunity to merge sustainable living with commercial success in a way that hadn't been done before.

This, of course, is not the end of the story. One thing we want to make clear is that *Be More Pirate* is not some kind of eye-patch-wearing unicorn that saves people from their fate after a few hours of reading. Let's not get too drunk on our own rum here. Jim's new-found sense of purpose did not cause TAKK Cap to become an overnight success, numerous obstacles stood in his way; his lack of experience as a fund manager, for one.

Over the course of the next year Jim explored different avenues to make the idea work, including using celebrity ambassadors, and the creation of a membership club for the fund. But amid all the excitement fuelling the project he kept coming back to something from *Be More Pirate*: the idea that real, radical change always comes from the fringes of society.

Ever since the hammock epiphany, surfers had been Jim's pirates: a counter-culture movement with a deep connection to the ocean that had gradually infiltrated the mainstream via anything from board shorts to Guinness adverts. Surfing was the key component that underpinned Jim's own momentum.

'The reason I'm passionate about surfing is that it connects me viscerally with the environment, it gives me an amazing sense of wellbeing. I think many of us have a deep void inside ourselves; we do

jobs that we pretend we like and spend money to distract ourselves. I think this is ultimately why the climate crisis is happening.'

So the TAKK brand evolved and Jim set up TAKK Surf as a sister movement for surfers to unite around climate change and raise money. The idea of building a movement alongside the fund appealed to Jim as it spoke to another pirate principle: scaling for impact, not growth. There are 35 million surfers worldwide, many with their own profiles and extensive reach. In a short space of time, Jim has already managed to gain support from several well-known figures in the surfing world and has set an ambition to build a surfboard out of ocean waste then take it on a journey around the world, passed on from surfer to surfer, wave by wave. As a movement, the potential for collective impact is enormous.

*'As surfers, we can be the agents of good and create positive change from the fringes. For too long the climate crisis has been doom and gloom; but, like our good friends at Toast Ale say: **If you want to change the world you have to throw a better party than those destroying it.'***

But the thing that strikes me about Jim's story most is why it has evolved over time. It's because he's shifted fully into a new, more pirate way of living and working. He's not following a business plan anymore; he's following his excitement. Sam and I often say to each other that 'the problem is the plan' because strict adherence to it can prevent a newer, better plan flowering as circumstances change or you learn new things. Part of the old way of doing things is a determination to cling to a plan for dear life even it doesn't make you happy or is difficult to undertake.

Becoming a pirate is an ability to let go, to shed old narratives, to freely admit you didn't get it right the first time, and be open to the next version of yourself and whatever emerges from that.

Refusing to walk the plank

Julie and Jim were undoubtedly aware that they weren't happy, but in the end they both had the privilege of making the decision to walk away and start afresh.

However, sometimes circumstances outside of your control are thrust upon you, and the change that's coming really doesn't feel like an opportunity, it feels like a disaster, and you don't know how the hell you're going to survive.

Becoming a pirate can therefore be less of an active choice and more of a flat-out refusal to accept an undesirable future that is arriving faster than you would have hoped. It's about picking up your (metaphorical) cutlass, even when the odds are *clearly* not in your favour, and fighting anyway. And from there something interesting can happen: a discovery that the status quo you thought you were fighting to save is:

a. The underlying reason for the crisis
b. Not all that great

The story that follows has all the vital elements that fuel piracy – a crisis which leads to clarity, purpose, and a new and exciting direction.

You will undoubtedly be aware of the concept of fair trade, but I'd hazard a guess that you probably have a mixed bag of knowledge as to what it does, and whether it is actually fair. I certainly do. I'd also hazard a guess that you haven't heard of a company called Traidcraft. Yet Traidcraft are pirates in the truest sense; a band of mavericks who rewrote the rules to make life better for people around the world. Founded in 1979, they introduced the first fair trade tea, coffee, and sugar to the UK, and in 1992 they co-founded the Fairtrade Foundation.[4] The mission was simple and radical: make capitalism fair.

For four decades they have successfully championed the need for just and sustainable international trade alongside their sister charity Traidcraft Exchange, watching quietly as the mainstream caught on and the now well-recognised Fairtrade mark spread.

4   www.traidcraft.co.uk/traidcraft-history

They continued to work out of their HQ in Gateshead, maintaining their own network of suppliers and loyal customers, yet behind the scenes CEO Robin Roth willingly admitted that their business model was unsustainable in the long term since Traidcraft were failing to consistently turn a profit.

Then, in 2018, they reached a breaking point. In the summer of that year, Robin brought the team together and laid out the situation. Unless they did something drastic, and quickly, the company would have to close its doors and cease trading. Livelihoods were at stake, not just for the Gateshead staff, but for their international suppliers. Traidcraft were facing then, what millions have faced in 2020 with Covid-19.

Jude Allen, Traidcraft's Business to Business Sales Lead, was only in her first year with the company when things began to unravel. By pure coincidence, Jude's husband had given her a copy of *Be More Pirate* at exactly the same time as a board member had given a copy to Robin. They arrived at very similar conclusions: with the company in crisis and half the staff at risk of redundancy, it felt like they had no choice. Go pirate or go under.

It was then that a small group of five staff got together and decided that Traidcraft, and all it stood for, was worth fighting for. Acting like a start-up (but with a 40-year legacy), they formed a radical new business plan, put it to the board and, when it was accepted, started work on getting it off the ground. Their first task was to look at streamlining – cutting back costs where necessary and focusing on the most profitable lines. The IT system was in desperate need of an upgrade too. But Robin and the core team knew that the problem ran deeper than these inefficiencies; it was something more intrinsic to Traidcraft's identity. They had lost sight of their story and their purpose.

Over the last two decades, competition from large online retailers had ballooned, and with it so had the ethical produce market which now has a much bigger focus on environmentalism. Fair trade, by comparison, had begun to look a bit old school and public interest and trust in the idea had diminished significantly. Robin said:

'Unfortunately, it is harder to be passionate about fair trade when even the most frequently boycotted and despised food multi-nationals have their token range of ethical products on the shelves. And in any case, what really is fair trade nowadays? What exactly are we fighting for? Ask 10 different people and you will get the proverbial 20 different answers.'

Traidcraft were no longer spearheading a trade revolution but rather trying to keep up. They'd lost their position as challengers at the edges, and internally everyone felt it.

'So, we began asking ourselves: Where is our passion? What will we fight for? We found that there were exactly three things we agreed on, which, given that there are 12 of us, came as a bit of a surprise. For example, we are openly, noisily passionate about equality: gender, sex, religion, regardless of background, heritage, experience or inheritance. However, it's possible to be in agreement with all of this but it is quite a different thing to fight for it. I think we are, by and large, a compromise-seeking nation not prone to outbursts of civil disobedience. Getting passionate is, quite honestly, a bit juvenile and awkward for friends and family to deal with.'

After sitting down together they found it easy to articulate what really mattered, but it wasn't translating into action. Everything from their tone of voice, imagery, and day-to-day work felt mismatched to their grander ambition of global trade justice. They realised that like many purpose-driven organisations, they had spent a long time nodding in agreement but refraining from any game-changing action.

How could they make that passion more real? First, they began looking around for examples of individuals and groups who were actually doing something radical. Examples emerged from the Communidad de la Paz (Peace community), an activist group in Northern Columbia who are bearing the brunt of regional conflict but use non-violent methods of resistance, and the climate scientists involved with Extinction Rebellion who are prepared to go to prison for their beliefs. Here were concrete demonstrations of people making sacrifices for their beliefs.

Everyone at Traidcraft felt that urgency and a keen sense of purpose lay at the heart of their original success, and reclaiming it was the secret to getting back on track. Purpose is what gives us clarity, resilience, and momentum in choppy waters; it is the stability we need when the system fails. In asking these questions about what they were fighting for, they'd discovered something fundamental: this wasn't just a fight to keep Traidcraft trading and in business, it was a wake up call to reinvent an organisation that had forgotten its roots.

Traidcraft committed to monthly Battle Line meetings to hold each other accountable to the idea of reinvention, even if they didn't yet know what that looked like. They returned to the challenges within the chapters in *Be More Pirate* as a lesson plan.

But even then, with a plan in place, they were fighting the tension between keeping the wheels churning and some money coming in, and taking the time to nail down what 'the new Traidcraft' would look like.

A new rallying cry

In February 2019, on a cold rainy night in Newcastle, four members of the Traidcraft team sat in the front row at a *Be More Pirate* event. Sam and I approached them afterwards to find out who they were and why they were so enthusiastic, which was when we learned of how they'd used the book to avert closure. Immediately, we offered to share the lessons we were learning from the community (that have become this book) with them.

In the summer, we went to their Gateshead offices and ran a workshop where we asked them to focus on shared values and stories strong enough to fight for. This was when we began to unlock the real potential. We worked through the team's individual ambitions and contributions and it was agreed that CEO Robin should be out on the road, talking and advocating regularly. We pushed him to define the practical steps – who would he be speaking to, where, through what mediums?

We then asked what exactly the new message was, as he saw it.

The answer prompted something completely unexpected: several minutes revealing a new mission statement that was far bigger and bolder than previously thought. Sam, the rest of the team, and I were left open-mouthed by Robin's reinvention of the purpose and purity of a new, stronger twenty-first-century Traidcraft mission. You could have heard a pin drop.

In brief, he said this:

'Seventy per cent of our food comes from small farmers in Asia, Africa, and Latin America, but the soil is being rapidly destroyed by climate change. If we do not rethink and democratise all of our supply chain systems now, in the next 30 years, the supermarkets will be empty. Traidcraft should lead the way.'

When asked why he'd not said this aloud before, he replied that he did not want to tell the team what to do. But once shared, the team replied that they believed in him all the more and were inspired to get behind this newly articulated and upgraded vision. It wasn't so much what he said, as how he said it. It was truth telling at its best, highlighting the best of Traidcraft: the deep knowledge they have of food supply chain systems and a global outlook. The facts he gave were scary and the mission felt almost impossible, which meant they had returned to their original place – the fringes.

The crisis became the catalyst. It was as clear as day that this new mission contained the energy they needed to see that Traidcraft was not only worth saving, but it could do something historic again.

The mutiny mindset: lessons learned

1. Listen to yourself. The inner rebellion is the first step. To stand up to power, first you have stand up to yourself. If we limit who we are by not listening to what we really want or need, it will limit what change we can achieve in the outside world.

What are you not giving yourself permission to do, say or be?

2. Crisis brings clarity. The spirit of piracy lives in the shadows. It is often born of failure and hardship, but we shouldn't always view this as something to shy away from. Rubbing up against something you fear can help to understand what is important. So how about inviting it in?

What is the most uncomfortable question you could ask yourself?
What are you avoiding, and why?

3. Know your own power. It is a myth to believe that power is only held in status, wealth or institutions. Power – our ability to do something – ultimately comes from within. But if we don't understand our individual source of power we will unconsciously give it away rather than use it to our advantage. So take the time to figure out where your power comes from.

What do you do effortlessly?
When do you feel most inspired?

*

When the seas are rough and everything is sliding around you, a strongly held belief in why you're doing what you're doing is about the only anchor you can really rely on.

The next step is to lay it down in lore.

Rise to You

With every tomorrow
And next time
And one day
And soon come
The sun grows tired of our waiting,
Our excuses and entitled patience
Our confidence in the second chance
That forever holds us from taking one

What if one day the night never comes
And the sun holds the sky hostage
And acted upon aspirations are the price to pay
For night to ever come again?
How many twenty-fours would it take
to give action to these ideas?

Pump action into you
Whether it's making that call or making that plan
The sun shines brightest on those who stand

– Sophia Thakur

Chapter Four

Live by the Code

I looked around and thought… I'm part of the problem. Stories of despair make us feel powerless. We wanted to better define what it is we're fighting for, rather than just repeating what it is we're fighting against.

Veronica Yates

Almost every nation state in the world has a government – a central authority that creates a set of rules by which its citizens are governed. This is the primary way we organise ourselves to ensure things happen and people stay safe. Yet it is not the only way, and it certainly may not be the best way.

Pirates did things differently. They didn't do government, but like any other group of people trying to survive, they still required a level of order and social harmony on board their ships. It would not have been possible to be as successful as they were without putting in place some rules to describe how they would live and work together – largely to prevent conflict. So they created their own form of governance: the Pirate Code.

The key difference between a code or pirate constitution and traditional government as a means to keep order, is that the code was created via direct democracy and was entirely voluntary. This is explained succinctly in economist Peter T. Leeson's excellent book *The Invisible Hook*. The articles that formed a code were created by a unanimous vote, *everybody* had to agree to them to reduce the risk of mutiny. So, while punishments were severe if you violated the code, every single pirate had voluntarily signed up to obey those rules. This is quite different to laws created by governments which are passed top down and enforced, even when large swathes of the population disagree or do not benefit from those laws.

Pirate Codes differed from crew to crew, but historians agree that most codes had core similarities that '...*emerged from piratical interactions and information sharing, not from a Pirate King who centrally designed and imposed a common code on all current and future sea bandits.*'[5]

If there's anything then that made pirates successful, it's the code. It was a way to operationalise their values and establish how to work together to achieve their goals. Every modern organisation has a version of how they express their identity and govern themselves, but they don't always work very well. This chapter explores why a Pirate Code is a useful form of governance, and the ways in which our modern pirates have begun replacing the usual tropes with a code of their own.

Policies vs values vs mission statements

Writing a Pirate Code is about closing the gap between intention and action. If every human being acted in accordance with what they say matters most to them, the world would be in a very different place. The pirate version of yourself is the best version of yourself; the one where you tell the truth, fearlessly, and act on what you believe in.

Pirates simply did not have the option to say one thing and do another. They couldn't afford to turn a blind eye to dead weights pretending to work, or petty politicking that might turn into a full-blown swordfight, so they had to be radically honest about human behaviour. The codes they created spoke to the reality of what they needed in order to survive, and, hopefully, thrive as a team.

5   p.60 *The Invisible Hook*, Leeson, Peter. T

Today we pretty much do the opposite. There's a reason why the BBC mockumentary W1A has a Head of Values as its protagonist: the word 'values' has become so meaningless in organisational culture that you'd be forgiven for glazing over and skipping this chapter. Most organisations have a delicate soup of policies coupled with brand values, internal values, and a mission statement that are barely distinguishable from those of its competitors.

Organisational values and mission statements tend to fall into these common traps:

- they were written by one or two people in the company (or worse, an outsider) on behalf of everyone else
- they were thought up to help the company feel and look a certain way to the outside world, so that they 'make sense' in relation to the rest of the sector.

If creating an organisational identity is simply a vanity project for external consumption and doesn't have buy in from the people actually doing the day-to-day work, there is no way it will help to navigate through trickier times.

A code, by comparison, is all about building culture. Culture is the reality of what actually happens in a workplace, a college, a place of worship or even a friendship group. What's spoken out loud and what's buried. It's what it *feels* like to be there. Policies do not build culture they only explain what to do when a particular situation arises. Similarly, for the reasons stated above, organisational values or mission statements rarely represent what it feels like to be at a place, despite brochures or PowerPoint presentations exuberantly claiming the opposite. So, because the usual blend of rules doesn't actively build culture, most of the time, a culture comes together by accident, based on the mix of people and some longstanding precedents.

Writing a code is about building culture – *explicitly*. And it's that last part that's really important. **It's not meant to be a one-day affair, it's meant to be an ongoing experience.**

The process of thinking about, writing, and saying your values out loud to other people regularly is an end itself. If you confine values to a document that you only look at twice a year, the rest of the time the *real* culture will prevail. It has to be lived, expressed, built out of what is actually happening on the ground, and get to the heart of what people care about.

A new standard for NGOs

The first time we received a detailed Pirate Code written by a twenty-first-century organisation, Sam nearly shit the bed in disbelief, to be honest.

That organisation was the Child Rights International Network (CRIN), a human rights NGO, who half-jokingly refer to themselves as a 'self-loathing charity'.

CRIN is led by Veronica Yates (up until the time of writing). In the middle of 2017, she came to some stark realisations about the charity sector and began asking serious questions:

- There are more charities than ever before, but inequality is growing – so what are we actually fixing?
- Are charities just acting as society's plasters, mending what we can and easing our guilt so we can carry on ignoring the root of the problem?
- Charities have to peddle narratives of misery to keep money coming in... can we be strong advocates while we're channelling and promoting negative stories?
- DOES ANY OF THIS FEEL LIKE A WELL-FUNCTIONING MODEL?

Veronica concluded that it does not.

'I looked around and thought... I'm part of the problem. Stories of despair make us feel powerless. We wanted to better define what it is we're fighting for, rather than just repeating what it is we're fighting against.'

During the process of reviewing the strategy and rethinking CRIN's role, Veronica read a lot of books and articles about how change happens, about movements, and the NGO sector, and the more she did, the more she felt they were going to become irrelevant unless they took a bolder approach to how they work and who they work with. She could see that many NGOs were struggling to stay afloat and had to choose between closing down or becoming reliant on project funding to exist. But CRIN didn't want to just take project funding if it meant compromising on their values and taking money from the wrong sources.

'To quote Be More Pirate, *we were not willing to simply "fund ourselves into existence".'*

When the time came to pen the new strategy, Veronica found herself paralysed. She really didn't want to write yet another boring five-year plan that only those who have to will read, and that says they are going to achieve x within y number of years – something that is always just wishful thinking.

'*That is when I came across* Be More Pirate *and the chapter about not writing business plans or strategy plans, but a code. This was exactly what we needed: something bold that would guide us in our work, and that would help us put into practice what we believe in – because what we believe in as individuals was what kept us in the organisation, this was our greatest strength.'*

The purpose of CRIN writing their code was to define what they stood for, but before we get into the details of that, how they arrived there in the first place is worth explaining. The last chapter showed that a point of crisis can be a catalyst for working out your purpose, but most of the time, we're not in that space. We're just ticking along, business as usual without any sense of urgency to change, until it's too late.

Knowing this, Veronica decided to try to recreate a psychological space for her team that was a bit closer to the urgency that pirates would have experienced by putting a scary proposition on the table. She got everyone together and asked them: should we even exist? Is it possible that our existence is not only maintaining the status quo, but actually making things worse?

In order to answer this question, together, they wrote a hypothetical exit strategy for CRIN. If they were to plan to shut down within six months, what would they do with all the current projects? What other organisations or charities could they give them to and was there anything unique that felt too important to give up on?

Two things came out of this exercise. The first was that as a team they were definitely not ready to give up.

'When we did our exit strategy, we all came to the same conclusion. What made us stand out in our field were our values, e.g. rights, not charity; that we believed in transparency, that we are stronger together, etc. We had about four or five back then that were written into our "this is who we are" description. And we practised them to some extent in our external interactions.'

Every single person said that the values of the organisation were one of the reasons why they believed in the cause and this included being unapologetic and willing to be a lone voice if it felt right.

'Our values and principles were not just PR language that we adopted to make us sound cool. We couldn't stand the growing trend in the corporate world of pretending they stand for something other than profit because it's cool to sound like you care about gay rights, girls' education or whatever cause a particular company felt isn't too controversial to sign up to.'

Secondly, it enabled some members of the team to see that their role should come to a natural end and they made the decision to leave. Collaborative redundancy – imagine that?

From this point, they were able to write the code.

They made a list of the values that they'd already agreed to, then all added to that list. As it grew and grew, they divided into smaller drafting teams of three or four for each article, so that they all worked on the same number of articles, but with different people. Each group then had to flesh out each article. Afterwards they compiled everything into one long code, did some more editing in groups, merging and reframing, until the final version emerged.

It's important to acknowledge, now, that each organisation writing their own code has approached it slightly differently, because every culture is different. The process is about understanding who you are, what you stand for, and what behaviours will make that a reality. Forget about what anyone else is doing. There is no formula – formulas and frameworks are binned.

'We see this is an ongoing process, where we will revisit the code as and when, rewrite it, add to it, etc. We have also begun smaller group discussions around specific articles where we feel we still have some ways to go to achieve implementation.'

The full version of the code can be found on their website. In a later chapter we'll look at exactly where it took them next.

The CRIN code

Part 1 – We have a mission
Rights, not charity
Children's rights, human rights
Justice, not compromise
Accountability, not apology
Diversity, not homogeny
We are Earth's custodians, not its owners

Part II – We have an attitude
Principles, not pragmatism
Critical thinking, not compliance
Feminism, not patriarchy
If you can't imagine it, you can't achieve it
Promote children's rights, not ourselves
Invest in failure, not quick wins

Part III – We have the means
Advocate in language, not words

Don't grow, network
Stronger together, not apart
Be open, not proprietary
Think ethically, be ethical
Safeguarding children, not the organisation

Principles vs protocols

An extremely advantageous side effect of a code is that it builds trust, but not for the reasons you might imagine. Yes, the process of working things out together does usually bond the team and create some trust, but it's also something about the nature of the code itself.

One of the reasons why it's so difficult to create trust is due to the kind of rules we usually have. They tend to be overly prescriptive – a list of do's and don'ts or 'protocols'. Telling people exactly what to do rather than simply explaining a problem or task suggests that you do not trust them to learn, interpret or use their own (probably quite good) judgement. Strict rules are a legacy of command and control organisational models. While you are still running things on this basis, a high level of trust is virtually impossible.

Putting trust in other people sounds risky... but is it? Does it just *feel* risky? Is it possible that even in high stakes environments, using broad principles that experienced individuals have to interpret, instead of an approach that tells people exactly what to do, can result in safer outcomes?

Safety requires vigilance and active engagement within your environment; when you are consistently told to be obedient and defer to an authority figure to make decisions, you lose the sense of responsibility and ownership of the problem. It feels utterly counter-intuitive to most of us, but simpler rules that are more like principles can work better.

Professor Andrew Sharman is the current President of the Institution of Occupational Safety and Health (IOSH), as well as a global consultant to Fortune 500 organisations on leadership and culture, and the author of several books on wellbeing and health & safety. He has been pushing people to think differently about rules for the last two decades.

'Globally, "safety" has been oversold. Thousands of companies – often led by committed CEOs or well-meaning H&S practitioners – have fetishised "zero accidents" targets and allowed regulation to drive policy, creating an over-reliance on paperwork. This is often accompanied by all manner of signage and marketing propaganda in a bid to make workers feel cared for, but essentially they all take the same approach – literally instructing people to "Be Safe!". But it just isn't working.'

Andrew came across *Be More Pirate* during a consultation with a client (the world's fastest Formula One team), where, at the start of the meeting, he was told, 'You've gotta start reading this.' Andrew picked up the book at the airport bookstore and read the entire thing on his flight home. Several weeks later he became part of the crew on board the *Golden Hinde* in London.

IOSH is the world's leading membership body for health and safety with over 48,000 members in 130 countries. It is the last place you might expect to take well to pirates, but under Andrew's leadership they are changing the narrative to help people understand that health and safety isn't about rules, but about culture. And once you go beyond the stereotypes, there are obvious lessons to be drawn from the way that pirates governed themselves.

'I hear a lot in my consultancy work that the rules are too difficult to understand, so people find shortcuts and ways to work around them. Paperwork, systems, and processes are only useful if they prompt people to think – and then do the right thing.

'For many leaders, safety has become about paperwork and procedures rather than doing the right thing, but attitude is the difference between an accident and excellent performance. My philosophy is to clean up the BS and get to what safety is all about: people.'

It may still *feel* scary to not be able to control everything around you – through the implementation of strict rules or otherwise –

but on a personal level, Andrew has taught himself to question this impulse. In his spare time, he dives with great white sharks – without a cage – as a way of evolving his own fear (of the water), because he believes the biggest risk of all is to allow yourself to be ruled by it.[6]

Be more 'parkrun'

One organisation that has figured out the link between simplicity, trust, and safety is the charity parkrun. It does what is says on the tin – gets people out running in parks, but it needs lots of volunteers to support the regularity. Managing volunteers is one of those areas where there is a tendency to go overboard on requirements and regulations in the name of safety, but parkrun is doing the opposite. Dr Helen Timbrell, former Director of Volunteering and Participation at the National Trust, is a parkrun Event Director and advocate of their approach:

'... *most of parkrun's volunteer roles have only have one-line descriptors. They are so free of a long list of requirements that people can basically start right away. It's not that they don't prioritise safety, but they have recognised that getting people involved is the main priority, and to do this, they have to trust that most people will be safe and use good judgement. It makes sense, in life and in work, most of us manage big responsibilities like teams and mortgages, and having families, and yet in volunteering, there can be an unhelpful tendency to mollycoddle and plan for failure. My husband is also a regular parkrun Run Director and often describes the parkrun ethos as simply "don't be a dick".'*

This message has become all the more significant in 2020 as organisations have needed to mobilise far more volunteers than usual in order to manage the coronavirus response. This will continue to be the case if in future we face further natural disasters as a result of the climate crisis. Getting essential supplies to vulnerable, isolated people is challenging if you have reams

6   See his TED talk for more on how this pirate reframes his perspectives.

of red tape in the form of ten-page risk assessments and DBS checks that can't be processed quickly enough. It is a moment when a simple code of conduct might be enough, especially if the alternative means people are not reached at all. Or at least we should be asking the question – what is the bigger risk here?

Going beyond principles

There's no better time to establish your code than when you are starting afresh, which is exactly what Robbie Greatrex did when he founded creative agency Mere Mortals in late 2018. After 15 years working in advertising, Robbie had built up a strong set of beliefs about how a creative agency should run and how it can be a force for good for its employees and for the planet. When he decided to strike out alone, the first task he set himself was to capture these beliefs and guiding principles for his new company in The Mortal Code.

Article #1. No Compromise
We live in a world of shortcuts and excuses where excellence has become a rarity, and good has become good enough. Well, sorry. We refuse to play along. At Mere Mortals we never ever compromise the quality of the work we produce. We challenge the mediocre, stand against doing the bare minimum, and despise the feeling of 'could have done better'.

Article #2. Drop the Attitude
Unfortunately, some people can be rude, arrogant, and disrespectful. They can be unpleasant to be around and a nightmare to work with. Not on our watch. At Mere Mortals we treat each other with total respect and expect no less in return.

Article #3. Don't conform
We're sick and tired of our industry's obsession with conforming to the same trendy, identikit culture. We break this mould. At

Mere Mortals we demand everyone just be themselves. Our culture isn't some prefabricated image for people to conform to. Quite the opposite.

Article #4. Step up to the plate

We're bored with micromanagement, inflated teams and multiple signoffs. We're too impatient to be stuck in training mode, and too ambitious to wonder 'what if'. We champion smart, ambitious, and spirited individuals who take risks and give things a go. We relish the challenge, trust our gut, and make decisions swiftly and decisively.

Article #5. See the Bigger Picture

Like it or not, profit-driven businesses play a huge role in the world around us, while people's happiness and the impact on our planet are often relegated to nice-to-haves. Screw that thinking. At Mere Mortals we care about our impact on people and planet. We volunteer, fundraise, and play a role in our community.

These five articles clearly outline the core values upon which the company was founded. This is what Robbie wanted: a code that is flexible enough to stand the test of time as Mere Mortals navigates through a rapidly changing world. But how do you ensure that, once written, your code is put to good use? How do you translate enduring beliefs into tangible action?

Robbie explains his approach like this:

'We sat down as a team and went through each of the five articles asking ourselves what they meant to how we operate day to day. For example, we say, "Step up to the plate", however, we quickly realised that to empower people to do so, we must show we trust them. A good starting point for this was to simplify our policies – things such as working from home, taking a taxi to a meeting, or buying a client lunch. Ours became incredibly simple: Use Good Judgement.'

The next step is to stress test your code on real-world experiences. **The articles are there to help you make decisions in**

hard times. Does it help you choose whether to go with client A or B? Will it help to decide how to recruit new team members? If a particular article doesn't naturally lead to action you should probably question the value of its inclusion. The article 'See the Bigger Picture' led Robbie to put in an application to become a B Corp so that he would then become accountable to their social and environmental standards.

A strong set of articles also states opinions, which The Mortal Code does in abundance. The idea behind this is that a good article should not be generic, it should be disputable in some way. There *should* be an argument to be had. If the articles don't represent opinion, they're probably a bit meaningless.

However, strong opinions can leave things open to misinterpretation. In Robbie's case, using phrases like 'no compromise' only work if everyone understands the parameters involved. What does it really mean to not compromise on the quality of work? You could interpret 'no compromise' as 'work harder' and end up slaving away all hours, or it could create a culture of presenteeism, so it's important to interrogate your articles and ensure your code is crystal clear.

'To ensure bold statements such as "no compromise" were not misunderstood, we took care to include other clarifying statements in other parts of the code such as, in this case, "We take happiness seriously and switch off after a hard day's work". It's a fine balance because you want your articles to be punchy, to stand for something, to state bold opinions. It's not easy, but when you do manage to strike the balance between a bold rallying cry and a practical guide for clear, consistent day-to-day actions it works wonders and sets you up for success.'

Don't be afraid to change the code[7]

For a code to really be a practical guide that informs the day-to-day work, you may have to write it more than once. This is a

---

7   This section was co-written with the Smiths' team

good thing. A robust code is not an unchanging mission statement that can be filed away and forgotten about. It's an evolving organism – evolving as you evolve. It's vibrant; it's important. Or it should be. Revisiting their Pirate Code regularly works for some crews. Other groups have revised their code in response to specific events.

Travel company Mr & Mrs Smith is a business straddling the tricky ground between start-up and global domination. They began as all good pirate crews do: as a ragtag bunch of passionate misfits dissatisfied with the status quo. Founders James and Tamara recognised that the existing hotel guides catered neither to people like them, nor to the new generation of independently minded boutique hotels that were springing up around the world.

'We came up with a proposal for a new kind of guidebook, researched it, wrote it, and took it to the publishers. Who didn't want it. Nobody wanted it.'

But they ran with the hunch, remortgaged the house, and published it themselves. Then, suddenly, everybody wanted it. Thanks to a handful of unconventional choices (including a guerrilla Who are Mr & Mrs Smith? fly-posting campaign around London, some distinctly voyeuristic cover photography, and the unlikely inclusion of a membership card in each copy to lure readers behind the velvet rope), the book was a runaway bestseller, laying the foundations – and setting out the brand values – of what has grown to become a multifaceted international travel club handling nearly 100,000 bookings a year.

In the beginning, being a pirate was easy for Mr & Mrs Smith. The company was a small group of talented individuals who were all personally invested in the success of what was first a gamble, then a brand. The hierarchy was flat and flexible; the best person for the job or the best team for the task would emerge organically when the need arose. Their founders were visible, accountable, and clearly involved in the day-to-day graft.

'Everyone understood and respected what their colleagues

brought into the mix and was humble enough to ask for help without embarrassment whenever they needed it. We were a textbook pirate crew.'

But, when you're growing quickly, it's easy to lose sight of the elements of the business that work and imagine that you have to constantly pursue something new in order to stay ahead. As a result, you risk losing the spark that was the reason for your success in the first place. Sam and I usually observe that when an organisation creeps over 40 people, the risk increases dramatically.

To an extent, it is a natural part of growth for almost every business; that small-team, everyone-is-invested, mix-and-match, together-against-the-world, start-up dynamism is almost impossible to maintain the larger and more layered your business becomes. Structures and protocols get put in place to guide company decision-making, offering less scope for individual risk-taking. Procedures have to be formalised to meet new starters' expectations (limiting spontaneity) and internal channels of communication are systematised (and the senior team appears to retreat further away from the frontline). With every efficiency measure comes another compromise until, eventually, you risk losing touch with your human and pirate roots. For Mr & Mrs Smith the impact of growth reached a turning point when something tragic and unexpected happened.

'We'd always been conscious of this process as we grew, but it was thrown into stark relief when a member of the senior team took their own life not long after joining the company. This was devastating, and transformative, for us. It forced us to stand still and reflect and, in the midst of the tragedy, we saw our team come together and look after each other in profoundly powerful ways. This was the beginning of a new framework for us, one that reconnected us to the company we'd been at our inception – a route back to our inner pirate.'

Be More Pirate first came to Mr & Mrs Smith via recommendation from one of their alumni – now a successful entrepreneur themselves. It seemed to come at exactly the right time, as a reminder of what they used to be, and gave them the tools to recapture some of that magic. They took from it a number of ideas to shape the 2020 Smith People Plan – an attempt to restore connection to their roots, set against the evolved landscape of a now-global business with great scope to develop further.

'We are now consciously implementing a Pirate Code – maintaining (and, where necessary, restoring) our flat hierarchy, working in a genuinely agile way, and ensuring we continue to learn and innovate. We don't think of this as "being more pirate" so much as "protecting our pirate". Not "Be More Pirate" exactly, but "Be Pirate, More".'

So far, the new measures they've introduced include:

- giving everyone a 'treasure chest' (a set amount of cash allocated to each person in the team) and the autonomy to decide what training, forums, workshops or whatever might enhance their professional and personal development;
- offering monthly sessions with impartial professional coaches;
- working with institutions such as the School of Life to help integrate emotional intelligence into departmental training;

…and they actively welcome suggestions from across the company for further initiatives they can collectively take. Everyone has a voice.

'We might not be fly-posting by night anymore, but we hope that rebellious spirit lives on in the work we do to further the brand.'

It's a balancing act, a recognition that these days they can't just wing it and hope for the best, nor can they fix every problem faced by every team member.

'But what we can do is remember where we came from, keep that disruptive flame alight, lead from the front, and do everything we can to look after all the bold and brilliant people who join our crew.'

Practising what you preach

...is really the essence of a code. So, we arrive back where we started – closing the gap between intention and action. When Sam and I first started working together we knew we ought to have a code of our own. We couldn't go around sounding off to everyone else without knowing ourselves that it worked.

And thank God we had a code, because without one I would've had absolutely nothing with which to understand success or failure. There was no other process, no set tasks, and very few things that absolutely 'had' to be done (this was deliberate). The whole job was an ongoing process of working out what was useful, what was exciting, and what would have an impact.

There were aspects of the new working style that I found difficult to get used to. It was only after about six months that I accepted our 'meetings' (even when I did write an agenda) were almost always going to be a long, meandering (often remarkable) conversation. The few times we did write something up, it was never revisited – things moved too fast. Eventually, I became more comfortable with the idea that writing something down is just a way to arrange your thoughts at a moment in time. It ain't the Bible, so let it go.

Still, there were periods when the absence of a plan really did feel like failure, even though I knew it wasn't due to disorganisation or a lack of commitment. It was mainly down to lack of manpower and an abundance of new opportunities. I never expected to do any public speaking but since the demand was there, I had to step up and go with it, which meant re-evaluating how best to use my time. I've since learned to accept this nerve-wracking blend of making it up as I go along with occasional divine intervention as a defining feature of my new work life. I managed to let go of the map and find a compass instead.

That compass was our code. It was the only thing that helped me to understand whether we were staying true to what we believed was important:

Article #1 Making a difference is more important than making numbers.

We agreed not to have any numerical KPIs (Key Performance Indicators), financial or otherwise, that would make it *look* as though something had been achieved. We were both committed to the idea that *Be More Pirate*, however it evolved, would put social impact first, not vanity metrics.

Article #2 To not fall into traditional work patterns or plan making.

Well, see above. Even though I found it disorientating, it was always our intention to avoid needless documents, formalities, and process.

Article #3 Have each other's back, but also call each other out.

When there's just two of you, the balance between support and accountability seemed crucial. We wanted to back each other and forgive mistakes, but not be afraid to point them out.

Article #4 To do one thing (at least) that changes the world.

From the outset we said we'd try to only focus on one or two things that would really have an impact rather than spread ourselves too thin.

Article #5 To have fun.

Otherwise, what's the point? If we're going to choose to be self-employed, set our own agendas and work really hard, it has to at least be fun.

Did it work perfectly? Almost. I'd say we got caught in the trap of doing a bit too much, but I also think it was inevitable that the first year would mean exploring lots of different avenues. I'm not sure it's possible to build a new network without keeping an open mind.

What we didn't anticipate was how we'd each react when things got tough. We hit a fracture after about nine months; a combination of fairly extreme workloads, travel, and personal circumstances that meant we stopped making the time to talk in depth, regularly. I felt like there was infinitely more pressure but far less support and admittedly I got really bloody angry at Sam because the 'having each other's back' seemed to have slipped away at a point when I really needed it. The worst part, though, was that I sucked it up. I did not try to reinstate the connection; I just resented the lack of it.

It turned out we were both making assumptions about what the other was doing and thinking, which created an unnecessary void in which we were both really lonely. The worst part of this was the dishonesty; the veneer of pretending everything's OK when it's the absolute opposite of how you feel. After a long and somewhat uncomfortable conversation during which we realised we were both daft and at fault, we added one more point to the code.

• To properly connect with each other once a week.

Actually, Sam did include this in the original job description, but we left it out of the code because it seemed almost too obvious and prescriptive. That was the mistake. Once you've been working together long enough and you understand what you value, it can be worth setting a firm practice or behaviour in stone, instead of just principles. This is reflected in the original Pirate Codes – some later articles *were* prescriptive, my favourite coming from the code of Captain John Philips which firmly dished out capital punishment to any pirate who forced themselves on an unwilling woman.[8]

8   P.65 The Invisible Hook, Leeson, Peter T.

Still, the most significant thing Pirate Codes did was to create rules about the rules. A code explained *how* they were going to make decisions, and this is more important than what the outcomes themselves are. It is precisely what allows you to stay steady and take appropriate action when the landscape changes.

Creating a code you want to live by: lessons learned

A Pirate Code is your compass to help you navigate through stormy seas. It's a way to create your culture on purpose. Every team creates their code in a different way, so there's no one singular question that nails it. Instead, here are a few points that we've found to work:

1. Have an opinion. As an organisation, team, or group of people – *what do you really care about?* What is the glue between you and what really sets you apart from others operating in the same space? Get to the heart of your values but ensure the statements you're making are authentic and unique to you. This is not the moment to hold back.

2. Set your ambitions. A code is as much about who you are now, as who you want to be. What's missing? What are you currently not doing, but think you should be? What would it make you really proud to achieve? If you made the papers (in a good way), what would it be for?

3. Does it feel motivating? A good code needs to resonate emotionally with you whoever your crew is, so think carefully about the words you choose. When you read them back, how do you *feel*? Excited? Inspired? The code should make you want to change the world.

4. Test it. Come up with a list of real-world scenarios – hiring, firing, paying people, collaboration, hierarchy, deciding your team's goals. Does your code help you figure out what to do when you're not sure? It's not about trying to make the decision that fits the code, but using the code to help you when you're confronted with a dilemma.

5. Revisit and update as you go. It doesn't matter if it's not quite right first time or needs revising; it is a good exercise to continually examine and re-examine values to see if they feel like a useful response to the world, especially if you ask – are we saying this because we think we ought to, or because we really believe it?

Chapter Five

Can You Be a Pirate in the Navy?

A failed attempt to make a change is always better than inaction, which we now know is the most heinous crime of our time.

Crystal Eisinger

In chapter three, I explained what it means to be a pirate in the context of this book and our movement. It felt important to do so because alongside the usual questions we get asked about Disney pirates and Somali pirates, there is also another group that has staked its claim on the word.

In the now infamous Steve Jobs quote, 'I'd rather be a pirate than join the navy,' which adorns the cover of *Be More Pirate*, Jobs positions the corporation as the navy, and himself and what would become Apple, as the ambitious challengers. Much has been written in the last two decades about the parallels between start-up culture and pirates – their agile nature, the ability to bend and break established norms and prototype something new. But, if we are truly drawing on the Golden Age Pirates as the original blueprint for what it means to be a pirate, then entrepreneurship, particularly that which is born and bred in Silicon Valley, is far too narrow to be the modern equivalent. And the corporation is too narrow a definition of the modern navy.

Yet it risks becoming the dominant story. Reid Hoffman, Co-Founder of LinkedIn, said this in conversation with Dara Khosrowshahi, the current CEO of Uber.

'You can tip from a culture that joyfully flaunts orthodoxy, to a culture that truly believes that winning is all that matters, and ethics be damned. And there's a second problem with piracy: It doesn't scale.

'This is why every start-up needs to shed its pirate nature at some point, and evolve into something more akin to a navy – no less heroic, but more disciplined, with rules of engagement, lines of communication, and long-term strategy.'[9]

The central misnomer here seems to be that pirates are willing to sacrifice ethics and discipline in the name of innovation and winning. But as we saw in the previous chapter, our pirates are fully grounded in their values, which more often than not represent fairness and equality – any and all innovation stems from there. Statements like the above from Reid Hoffman, once again equates pirates with greed and chaos, rather than equity and collaboration.

In fact very little about this discussion of pirates vs the navy felt accurate. Sam and I have witnessed quite the opposite: clear rules of engagement, strong lines of communication, and – most importantly – accountability, are actually much harder to maintain as you scale. Not because the channels aren't there, but because usually, scale means increased hierarchy and a greater distance between people. Over time this creates large gaps in communication and understanding, less collaboration between the people at the top and the bottom, and generally, less transparency.

Nevertheless, seeing this conversation play out raises an important question about who are the pirates and who is the navy? We have heard the word navy being used to describe not just large corporations, but the government, the state, the 'establishment' or 'the system'. However, my understanding from working with our pirates, is that the defining feature of a navy is not structure, size, order or discipline; it's power. A navy represents a concentration of power, and pirates always sit in opposition to that. As companies grow, power and wealth tend to be concentrated among few people,

9   mastersofscale.com/dara-khosrowshahi-how-pirates-become-the-navy

so the question of who are the navy, and can you be a pirate within it, depends on where you think power lies.

Previous generations used to refer to 'the system' or 'the man' and mainly mean government, but today, exponentially wealthy companies that have access to vast amounts of our data and are without democratic constraints, arguably hold more power. Apple remains innovative, but by this definition they are also very much the navy. The advertising industry is another good example of a space that is creative, and seen to be innovative, but holds a lot of power because of its ability to distract, persuade, and shape public opinion. And within it there will be companies like Robbie's in the previous chapter, who are pirates on the inside.

So in short, of course you can be a pirate in the navy because we all exist within a navy to some extent, it's just that depending on where you are, the idea of the navy may feel more present. Working inside a big corporation while trying to be a pirate is certainly more challenging, but it can also mean there is more ground to be gained, as we shall see in the story to follow.

It starts with us

The first risk in taking Be More Pirate into any corporate environment is that it is seen as a gimmick. If you're an employee in a global legacy organisation that has decades' worth of entrenched culture and protocol, even at a senior level, you might think that pirates are just something 'fun' to hook an away day onto, rather than a serious lever for change.

Mercedes-Benz would usually fall into this category. Owned by multi-national German automotive corporation Daimler, they're about as corporate as it gets and have long been viewed as a traditional luxury brand – well captured by their slogan 'the best or nothing'. But in the last few years the future has begun to feel less predictable, and with significant pressure to re-imagine greener modes of transport, business as usual at Daimler has become more and more difficult to maintain. As a result, some employees have started to find their courage because, really, Be More Pirate or Be Kodak and sink into the icy depths.

The pirate captain in this story is Nicola Burnside, Head of Marketing in the Mercedes-Benz vans team, based in Milton Keynes. From the beginning, Nic had a challenge on her hands. Although she'd managed to recruit a young, talented, forward thinking team, she was finding it increasingly hard to keep them on board. The team retained something of an underdog status; while the Mercedes brand is a household name, the vans section is outspent by their nearest competitor, so they're not exactly heralded within the company. Marketing too, is not a well-understood concept within the scope of the business, the traditional focus has always been hard sales. On top of that, the level of red tape around what they can and can't do is – dare I say it – unprecedented, so their ability to take risks and strike out with a new strategy requires pirate-like strength of character which luckily Nic has in spades. She saw an opportunity for changing the company culture and seized it.

'Daimler had recently landed some new internal values, one of which was "pioneering spirit," and after hearing Sam talk and then reading Be More Pirate, *I could see that there was a chance to reshape the culture.'*

Despite all of the obstacles, the vans division of Daimler is one of the most forward looking parts of the business which was why Nic invited Sam in to run two Be More Pirate sessions in parallel: one with just her team, and one across the rest of the business.

Within Nic's team, they started off by creating their code. When you're small and starting out it makes sense to use the code to inform exactly how the business will be run, but when you're part of a huge machine, it's unlikely you can change the mechanics overnight so the code has to serve a different purpose. What you're really looking for is a new spirit. The key here is to ensure that it resonates with the team on an emotional level. It needs to have the feel of 'oh right, *that's* who I am supposed to be.' Its primary function is to motivate everyone.

Unlike other codes, Mercedes kept theirs minimal – a series of short statements – but the one that really stuck was this: 'It starts with us'. This single, short sentence sums up what agency, independence, and risk-taking meant for them, and captures the feeling of permission they needed. As outlined in the previous chapter, a code is less about ending up with a lengthy document and more about the process of creating culture through consensus. It was significant enough that in a company as big as Daimler, Nic's team could set their own culture rather than having it set for them.

Mutiny

But, in order to really enact their ambitions, they needed buy in from the rest of the business. This is where pirates rub up against the navy and where the idea of mutiny really comes into its own, so it's worth explaining briefly exactly how a Be More Pirate workshop facilitates that. When Sam went in to run the workshop at Mercedes-Benz the goal was to facilitate a 'controlled' mutiny. It's a method he stumbled upon by accident but has the capacity to shift power dynamics from the navy to pirates, within a few hours.

After running through a series of provocations to support teams to think about their ambitions and where the barriers in the business lies, the goal of the workshop is ultimately to write some new rules, just as the Golden Age Pirates did. The whole room is then split into small crews, usually between six and eight people, of mixed levels and perspectives, and tasked with writing at least one new rule each (the longer you have to do this the better). Then, one by one each crew is required to stand up and declare it to everyone else. The rest of the room is then asked to also stand up if they agree and want to back this new rule. So long as there is a majority consensus, the crew has now gained permission to take it forward. Senior management or any other objectors cannot stand in their way, because permission has been given to try it out for a set period. The measure of success is whether the new rule sticks and others follow.

In the session with Mercedes something happened which is not uncommon: a standoff between the pirate crew proposing their suggestion, and a few senior people who objected and declared a right to final sign off. It's the delicate moment where the transference of power hangs in the balance. In this case, the battle was over culture. The team's new rule was about instilling a culture of being able to speak out and challenge, so it was ironic that the objections came in the form of trying to silence them.

This is when it is useful to have an external facilitator to ensure that the crews are seen and heard, and that the redistribution of power occurs. With Sam's intervention, the crew were allowed to hold the space and continue with their challenge. It was this that turned the tide for Mercedes, because it was a moment when they realised that pirates *can* win this, and things could actually change. And as a lesson in leadership, the senior people in opposition won a lot of respect from the team because they did back down and acknowledge that maybe they did not grasp the full extent of the problem.

The remaining new rules put forward were largely technical, relating to logistics, red tape, and insurance. Most of the crews wanted independence and permission to take risks so that they could do a better job. With the tension of the earlier moment dispersed, the senior leaders, who would have previously tried to impose more control, decided instead that they could turn their usual heavy handedness outwards instead, towards their Stuttgart HQ, and provide air cover for the team as they broke a few of the internal rules.

Permission granted

So, what next? Having embraced a Pirate Code and witnessed senior management embrace a more pirate approach, Nicola's team set about creating an entirely different marketing strategy, one that seemed counter-intuitive but instinctively felt like the right way to go. Approaching this as pirates meant starting from the opposite end of the spectrum. Rather than try to outpace their competitors on media spend as they usually would, they decided to try to *understand the customers* with a sharp focus on small businesses. Rather than use TV and other advertising to broadcast a message that reinforced the image of a distant luxury brand, they'd aim to build relationships.

They began by mapping out all the networks of entrepreneurs as well as small and medium-sized businesses across the UK. Then, one rainy day, they took to the road to start meeting them. It is certainly not common for the marketing director of a big brand like Mercedes to spend their time this way, but Nicola knew that basing all their decisions on data handed down from ad agencies wasn't getting them where they wanted to be. The vans team's corporate mission statement had always been to 'keep business moving' and now they were actually listening to what it takes to keep business moving. The new story was about how they could genuinely support the infrastructure of SMEs in the UK, so they started speaking to networks like Impact Hub and Enterprise Nation. One of the first things they did was support a conference for female entrepreneurs. Given that the whole of the automotive industry is still male dominated, actively building relationships with minorities within their minority customer base was a bold and rare move.

Meeting the customers also gave Nicola new power. She now had insights that no one else in the business had. Building these relationships helped them gain new perspectives on what their customers wanted and needed, and she could take these into every meeting and use them as necessary leverage. Their approach was still met with some initial resistance, in part because it's unlikely to translate into the same return on investment as other types of marketing – at least not in the short term. But Nic has the backing of MD Steve Bridge who understands and supports the vision and is keen for vans to lead the charge inside Daimler and set new precedents for the future of the business. The new goal is not to sell blindly, but to sell wisely through deep understanding of what their customers need. They're not making a song and dance about the strategy, but quietly proving that it works. The moment to fly the flag will come, for now the long-term goal is to build a community out of their customers, which, in a company like Daimler, will be a first.

*

Another kind of navy

In his 2013 essay *On the Phenomenon of Bullshit Jobs* anthropologist David Graeber writes:

'Huge swathes of people, in Europe and North America in particular, spend their entire working lives, performing tasks they secretly believe do not really need to be performed. The moral and spiritual damage that comes from this situation is profound. It is a scar across our collective soul. Yet virtually no one talks about it.'

Hallelujah. The truth, at last. This essay, unsurprisingly, went viral and has since become a book. What Graeber is describing is the sad state of modern office work, particularly in large organisations. We go to the same place day in day out, mostly at the same times. The day is spent staring at a screen and reactively responding to emails, which takes up more time than it should – or we let it, because it feels tangible in lieu of any greater sense of purpose. We fill those emails with sentences that say anything but the truth. We then go to meetings that result in little change. Afterwards, we create PowerPoint presentations filled with metrics that describe what has been done rather than what has been *achieved*. We make talking about work, the work itself.

This situation, as Graeber accurately describes, has become tyrannous, and is a new navy of sorts. We feel incredibly busy, but what is it all amounting to? Twenty-first-century clutter, as I'm going to term it, extends far beyond just our work lives too. How many new online courses, classes, newsletters or other sources of entertainment have you signed up to in the last year, but never returned to? How many different apps? How many passwords do you have but need to regularly reset? How many series on Netflix do you feel you ought to have watched to not feel like a cultural caveman? We are on the receiving end of an endless stream of new products, and our personal lives are heckled by interruptions masquerading as improvements and essentials. The more incoming stuff, the more we respond, but the majority of it is neither fulfilling nor useful, it simply steals our power.

The very first time I did a workshop with Sam, I sat with a group of three guys in their mid-twenties. When we got to the point where they were asked to define a rule they want to break, one spoke up hesitantly and said, '*It's not exactly a rule, but I really want to leave this WhatsApp group*'. The stream of chatter from a group of school friends that in real life he had drifted away from, created an ongoing, unimportant, and distracting task, and yet he was distinctly apprehensive about leaving altogether. I asked why, and he replied that he didn't want no contact at all, he just didn't want it nonstop. But, like most of the clutter we've become accustomed to, it simply snuck quietly in the back door...

Clear the decks

Plenty has been written on the benefits of simplification and doing less so it's not a new idea that we're introducing, yet we've observed that it doesn't seem to be happening. It really doesn't matter how many smart people have already diagnosed the problem; it matters whether we are acting on it. And if not, why not?

Pirates are a useful bunch to draw on here because they didn't have the opportunity to dither among a cacophony of different options, they figured out who could and wanted to do what, and acted swiftly. It might sound like the simplest piece of advice but clearing the decks of process or excess life admin is one the most effective things any person can do to begin rewriting the rules. As I outlined at the beginning, challenging the status quo is hard work and you simply won't have the capacity to see it through if you're beholden to a near full diary or inbox, so this is a significant, preparative step.

The lead pirate in this next example is the formidable Crystal Eisinger. Crystal is Head of Marketing, Strategy and Operations at Google UK, a Forbes 30 under 30 leader in media and marketing, and in her spare time a co-host of the podcast *Greater than 11%* and an award-winning fisherwoman. But despite all the accolades, she is refreshingly frank about her own and her team's pitfalls.

'Be More Pirate *grabbed me by the collar, shook me, and rather embarrassingly and unapologetically highlighted to me that I was the only thing standing in the way of making great things happen. Sometimes it works, sometimes it doesn't but a failed attempt to make a change is always better than inaction, which we now know is the most heinous crime of our time.*'

To our delight, Crystal has taken pirating metaphors to new heights in order to capture a sense of the weight of all those pointless tasks that drag us down.

'*If organisations are great ships headed towards, well, somewhere, the accumulation of process, meetings about meetings, working groups, offsites, team seating arrangements, expenses, working from home policies, non-financial rewards, and team meeting agendas are the barnacles which ultimately slow the ship down and make it less aqua dynamic. And boy, do those barnacles try to cling on for dear life and no they're not the glamorous things to talk about but they are crucial to pave the way for creativity, innovation, and action.*'

An increase in 'stuff', the 'barnacles on your ship' or however you might want to put it, is somewhat inevitable as a company expands. However, much of the excess activity within business occurs because we wrongly equate more output with more work and therefore more success. Especially when there is a legacy expectation of having something to show. This problem is surprisingly widespread, even with companies you'd imagine having their productivity down to a T.

In every workshop session Sam and I run, we ask the question, 'What do you allow to get in your way?', one of the original questions in *Be More Pirate*. The reason why we ask, is to shift the perception of what you actually need to do next. For example:

Goal: engage the public in your latest product
Task: create an exciting campaign for the product
Obstacle: already big to-do list, not enough time/head space available to tap into optimum creativity
Real task: attack some of the barnacles that are in the way.

The problem is that everyone wants to jump in and work on the campaign straight away, because it feels more important at face value and will definitely be more fun.

'One of the most difficult things about clearing away the barnacles is that often barnacles are banal and don't make great topics for offsites. For example talking about billing systems, or legacy processes that are knotty and hard to undo. Clearing a barnacle can often involve 25 emails and an uninterested leadership group because the topic is highly unstrategic but nevertheless slows the team down. Taking time and effort to scrape those barnacles off the boat will be one of, if not your biggest critical success factor in driving change.'

Make it about behaviours and mindset instead

In March 2019, Crystal was responsible for launching a new sales team within Google. Determined not to give the barnacles any space to settle in, she imagined how they could break the usual rules and set up differently. So, they didn't spend weeks and weeks mapping out roles and responsibilities, or hours locked in a room wordsmithing and figuring out the mission statement. Instead, they focused on behaviours and mindset. They launched a team purely on a set of behavioural expectations, focusing on the 'why' and the 'how'… trusting that they had a team of smart people who would figure out the 'what'.

The launch event demonstrated their approach. The sales director did not present a 50-slide presentation full of org charts and platitudes peppered with the usual sporting metaphors.

Instead, he told a story about his mental health challenges, showing it was OK not to be OK and asking the team to aspire to greatness, but not at all costs.

In the space they cleared, something more real was able to take root.

The experiment culminated in a set of values that live on in the team, which is now thriving from a cultural and commercial perspective one year on.

'There has been a continued cadence of inclusive activity to keep culture and behaviours at the forefront of this team which has served them incredibly well throughout Covid and also means that when it comes to moments like Mental Health Awareness Week the Sales Director has a real authenticity behind efforts rather than it being a burst of activity just for one week.'

Crystal emphasises that the easiest way to undermine momentum is having a bold vision but no concrete steps to remove the blockers that stop you from getting there. This is a key differential between working within a big navy-like organisation, versus working somewhere smaller and more pirate. There tends to be more barnacles on navy ships not just because they're bigger but because process and structure is usually a form of control. The first step inside a navy is often an exercise in doing less or letting go, but *how* you decide to let go, can also be via a much needed challenge to power.

'Clearing blockers is a crucial component of being more pirate and while they may not seem heroic, true transformation takes place in small, brave acts of resistance which start as simple as not turning up to a meeting or simply saying no.'

Small, brave acts of resistance are exactly where we will go next.

Working within the navy: lessons learned

1. Redistribute power: the biggest challenge of working within the navy is an unequal distribution of power which results in a culture of fear and limitation. So start by thinking about where power sits and how it could be reclaimed or shifted. For Mercedes, creating a team code put wind in their sales and led to a change in marketing strategy. The insights they gained from customers by actually spending time with them gave Nicola new power. Equally, rather than strip the leadership entirely of their power, they were called upon to use it differently – to challenge their HQ in Germany and provide protection to the UK team as they took a few more risks.

2. Clear the Decks: the second problem is too much clutter. Identifying what to do, in order to achieve a goal, first requires identifying what not to do. Standing in the way of greatness is usually a myriad of time-consuming to-dos that are easy to accomplish but do not further your real ambitions. Stopping is harder than starting, so *what could or should you stop doing?*

3. Replace 'doing' with 'being': the reason why a navy feels like a machine is because of the endless churn of doing, with little attention to 'being' as the driver of results. Rather than creating goals based solely on tasks and outputs, create a set of behavioural expectations. This is useful when a full-on Pirate Code feels too radical for a corporate environment. You could start small and simply focus on new behaviours within the context of one regular meeting, or in creating a new role, or via annual appraisals. It is a powerful way to subtly shift the culture.

PART THREE

Rewriting the Rules

Chapter Six

Small Bold Actions

We don't need nice people just saying it's 'process'. We need nice people who are willing to stick their head above the parapet and get shot.

Isaac Samuels

Isaac, quoted above, is one of the pirates who attended our networking event in the hidden warehouse in September 2019. On the night he gave a short speech to the audience to explain why he felt that his experience of the health and social care system over the last two decades had been so poor.

When I heard it, it reminded me of a sentiment spoken by Black Sam Bellamy, one of the heroes from the Golden Age, often referred to as the Prince of Pirates. In Black Sam's famous description of how the establishment legitimises the criminalisation of pirates, while justifying its treatment of the poor, he says this:

'They vilify us, the Scoundrels do, when there is only this Difference: They rob the Poor under the Cover of Law, forsooth, and we plunder the Rich under the Protection of our own Courage.'

Isaac draws a line to modernity by describing how the current rules of the day – what we might call due process or the systemisation of work – aren't simply annoying clutter, they actually provide a shield of legitimacy that allows people to kid themselves that they are doing the right thing, when what they ought to be doing is the brave thing. If you've ever heard the line 'I'm just doing my job', you'll know what I mean.

The antidote that we prescribe to the litany of stuff that clogs up the system: a definitive way to break the patterns of monotony, inertia, and righteous box ticking that don't actually support the outcomes we want, is to find a small, bold action. Something you could do tomorrow that is on the edge of what feels comfortable. It should be simple enough to execute in a reasonable time frame, not involve lots of other people or be logistically complex, but not feel easy either.

Small bold actions are what emerged from the first principle in *Be More Pirate*: Rebel. The call to break a stupid rule. You might have written a code or had a stab at creating some new rules, but for whatever reason, you're still collectively falling back into old ways of doing things and you need something to snap you out of it.

This chapter is about further defining the nature of the action we need, to really be more pirate.

Flex the rule-breaking muscle

Small bold actions are worthwhile because, frankly, even if it feels like a minor act of resistance at the time, you have no idea where it could lead. This was ultimately the case with Greta Thunberg consistently skipping school. If the action is simple, universal, and repeatable others are more likely to follow.

Remember Traidcraft from chapter three? In November 2019 they decided to boycott Black Friday which, given that all their sales are crucial, felt like a bold move. But they wanted to make a statement about consumerism: that we have to start putting quality over quantity and being more vocal about it. Traidcraft openly and actively, perhaps controversially for an e-commerce business, promote the message that 'the key to buying less, is buying right; investing in what is good, rather than chasing what is cheap'.

Granted, they're not the only company to do this, but the more that do, the less likely it will stay commercially acceptable to create mass selling hysteria and encourage people to buy things they do not need. Boycotting Black Friday wasn't difficult to do. In fact,

Traidcraft didn't have to do anything, except write a press release. It was actually minus work. Instead, they chose to spend the day in the local community, running a free refreshments and toiletries station at Newcastle Cathedral and creating an allotment in their office grounds.

One example sticks in my mind from a talk I did last year. When I asked the group what rules they might want to break, a woman who had spent her life working in HR declared that she didn't like writing 'competitive' as a substitute for actual figures when they advertised jobs. *'People deserve to know what they will get paid when they make the effort to write an application.'* (I'm paraphrasing, but it was along those lines.) Replacing this word with, at the very least, an actual salary range, was an action that she could both control and justify, the only real obstacle was fear of her line manager's reaction.

In another session, a manager (I'll call him Ben) in charge of internal communications said that he never asked their CEO to contribute to the internal newsletter because there was a precedent, set by his predecessor, not to bother him. Ben had accepted this and it had become a norm, but as a result, the CEO had become a distant 'too busy' figure, which was having a subtle but distinctly negative effect on the culture. Feedback from staff suggested they would welcome a few words of encouragement, guidance or self-reflection from their leader. So, from that point on, Ben pledged to ask the CEO for a few lines every single week.

Small bold actions are about realising that:

a. There is always something you can do
b. The impact may be much bigger than you imagine

It needn't always be a challenge to authority; it could simply be a challenge to yourself to put something on the line and break away from following instructions. A small bold action could just be a strategy to wake yourself up.

Another pioneer of small bold actions is Matthew Cook, one

of the crew aboard the *Golden Hinde* who shared his rebellion with the crowd. For the past 10 years, Matthew has been going to crowded public places and holding up cardboard signs inscribed with positive messages in a bid to cut through London's chronic loneliness and reinforce human connection. Written in bright coloured crayons they say things like 'you are beautiful' or 'have a lovely day'. He often takes them onto the tube trains, injecting the depths of the underworld with a bit of light.

'I remember the first time that I stood at the end of the train carriage and unfurled my sign. My hands were shaking so much that you probably couldn't even have read what was written. I didn't know how people would react and I was bracing myself for the worst, expecting to feel embarrassed and ashamed for doing something so far out of the ordinary. I found instead that putting myself out there was far more rewarding than it was terrifying.'

As a result of telling the *Golden Hinde* audience about it, he was able to recruit a few more pirates to his crusade, documented on @abeautifulsomething.

So you get the idea of what a small, bold action might be. However, as we dive deeper, the difference between what is 'bold' what is 'risky' becomes more pronounced because it is entirely dependent on context. We all have a different tolerance for what feels bold, new, and different; the rebellions of some may look tame, and not fit your own definition. But, don't judge others by your own parameters because their small bold action may just be the testing ground for something greater. As discussed in the previous chapter, being a pirate within a controlling environment is obviously more difficult, but it is possible to see out big ambitions by using a series of small bold actions to get there.

Captain Birds Eye meets Blackbeard

Most people know Birds Eye for two things: fish fingers and peas – a stellar combination that has graced kitchen tables for several decades. In 2015, Birds Eye's European branch was acquired by

Nomad Foods, merging with Findus and Iglo; suddenly the UK team were part of a much larger, global operation and change was coming from inside and out. The new food landscape is increasingly confusing, both for producers and consumers, and getting the balance right between cost, health, taste – and what's right for the planet as well – is changing fast.

What you need is a pirate on the inside.

Alex Dobson is a brand strategist and all-round great bloke who, after several years of working with well-known brands like Unilever, RBS, and Kellogg's, joined Nomad's commercial team in September 2018. About three weeks into the job, he found himself in Scotland on the Isle of Iona where, in a moment of downtime, he chanced upon hearing about *Be More Pirate* on Ed Milliband's podcast *Reasons to Be Cheerful*. He promptly downloaded the audiobook to listen to on the drive back to London.

Nine hours after leaving the island, Alex continued driving beyond his final destination just so that he could keep listening.

'I didn't realise how much I wanted to hear this message.'

Although new in the post, he felt certain that *Be More Pirate* would give the company an injection of the rebellious spirit required to tackle a challenging year ahead. Alex had spotted an opportunity to try to change people's perception of frozen foods which are, in fact, a healthy and sustainable way to eat good value food, yet tend to get lumped into the convenience food category. His team had also been tasked with a bigger mission: to come up with a new innovation for a frozen fish product – something that could rival fish fingers. No easy feat.

But Nomad faced the same problems outlined in the previous chapter. They were overwhelmed by their own schedules which made their ambitions feel daunting, not exciting. The small bold actions they needed had to be ones that enabled them to clear the decks first.

Here are a few of the new rules they came up with:

Meeting-Free Mondays – adding mountains more work

on the first day of the week is a bonafide recipe for stress. They decided to test this for three months with the senior team leading the way.

Be Here Now – no mobile phones in meetings. No more distractions. Let's stop pretending that multi-tasking was ever useful to anyone.

Readiness to act – which translated to a willingness to 'kill' things quicker if they're not working or don't feel right, and to follow more of an 80:20 mindset (the Pareto Principle; recognising that the good creative stuff only ever comes from 20% of the effort).

Embrace the power to say no – the senior management agreed that it was OK to say no to new incoming work or tasks if they're not as important as what you're already working on.

FuckIt Time – allowing everyone a few hours each week for proper uninterrupted time to think and reflect, rather than react.

1 in 1 out – an acceptance that something has to be dropped if new work comes in. The to-do list is not allowed to keep on growing forever...

An important function of small bold actions can be to provide momentum where it was previously non-existent. In this respect, if you come up with a whole list of ideas, start by ordering them so that the most achievable ones are actioned first. Other than that, we have since learned that there are three key features that make a small bold action successful:

1. It must fit within the 9–5 (or whatever your work hours may be): in some of the very early workshops we did, people would write new rules that involved creating entire new streams of work for themselves because they were trying to take on a monumentally big problem. It can happen when there's a lot of ambition and appetite, but the obvious risk is drowning in more work. Instead build the change into what already exists, and try to find the sweet spot where ease of execution meets maximum frustration levels.

2. It must be repeatable: if it's a one-off, chances are it will be treated as an exception and not a new rule, so find something that can be enacted regularly and by the majority of the team so that the behaviour compounds over time.

3. It has to feel a bit scary: this is the pirate piece, which makes it different from simply forming new habits. If your action is not bold, there is a greater chance of becoming uninterested. It needn't be something that gets you in trouble, but it needs to be out of sync with what's considered the norm.

If the suggestions that emerge as a result of point number three feel a bit too uncomfortable… that's where the mutiny comes in. Like Mercedes, the key lever at Birds Eye was that the team created each new rule together in small groups. The whole purpose of the mutiny format is to enable a bolder action than usual by creating **collective permission** to do things differently, and therefore collectively sharing the burden. It disables the fear element of having to be the only one who enacts the change.

For example, we've probably all heard some semblance of 'it's fine to fail' uttered from the lips of a leader at some point because, of course, theoretically, there is much learning to be gained from failure, but no one really wants to be the one modelling that. Just as captive animals don't bolt as soon as the door opens, we want to know that it's actually safe first. As Crystal at Google put it:

'…when a team is communicated one message from leadership, but sent organisational signals to the contrary, nothing but stasis ensues and stasis = rot.'

What Birds Eye were trying to do was change the culture from being one where maintaining an appearance of absolute busyness has long reigned supreme, to one that was genuinely productive. By finally having a truthful discussion about the (unrealistic) expectations around how much it is possible to really do well and still keep all aspects of your life in balance, they gave themselves collective permission to say no to more work. As a result, the fear of looking inefficient or incompetent dissolved.

Measuring success

Did their new rules succeed long term? I asked Alex this directly about six months after the workshop, with a suspicion that the answer would be 'yes and no'. He admitted that, yes, meetings do still sneak in on Mondays, but they have cut down the time frame significantly and the fact that people are aware of the too-many-meetings culture as a problem, has changed how they are approached. This did not feel like a betrayal of the pirate spirit, but closer to the truth of it. It didn't feel right to be rigid. Ironically, the measure of whether a culture has changed is signalled by less of an attachment to the usual metrics. Have you had any meetings on a Monday... well, who's counting?

The 6th R... resilience?

There is of course no guarantee that your rebellion will have the desired effect. It is up to you to decide whether the risk is worth the possibility of change and hopefully the coming chapters will provide some additional ideas on how to balance the risks with the potential rewards. It would, however, be wrong not to acknowledge that it can take an emotional toll. Crystal at Google spoke openly about this:

'For all the great things that acting like a pirate can achieve, nothing quite prepares you for the anxiety the night before, the feeling of your heart in the top of your throat before you step into that meeting and the overwhelming dread that what you might be saying or doing is going to ruin the credibility you've worked so hard to build up.'

She explained that she manages the exhaustion, anxiety, and discomfort she experiences in always being the 'difficult woman' by reframing it as growth. A small bold act of rebellion isn't always about the impact on the world around you, even if that's what you're shooting for. It's about the impact it can have on you. How it can change you.

Crystal also confessed this:

'There are times where you feel compelled to call bullshit and you end up looking like a twat. I'd be lying if this wasn't the case. This happened when a topic that is close to my heart was being discussed at a senior level and I was extremely disappointed with the output from a working group. So, full of conviction, I asked to speak to a very senior person within the business and expressed that I thought the work was inadequate.

'My observations were met with questions about what I would do differently given the complexity of the challenge and I didn't have good answers, and neither did I think I should have. Would I do that again? Probably not because I felt like it dented my credibility with that person. On positive days I feel proud that I said something and don't think my inability to come up with a solution on the spot reflected badly on me. On more self-critical days I think I just looked like an uninformed pain in the arse.'

This reflection struck me as even more valuable. Part of the reason we're afraid to take risks, is because (as discussed above) there are so few stories where failure for failure's sake is really a good thing. We commonly hear about failure only in the context of how it paved the way to success. But actually failing for the sake of showing others that the world doesn't end, that it's normal, and that even the smartest and most successful people make bad calls, might encourage us all to stick our necks out a bit further.

So that is the pirate prescription. Choose one slightly risky thing to do, raise your Jolly Roger, and get noticed. It gets easier the more you do it. The risk of not taking the small bold action is that someone else will, and you will be left with a feeling of knowing it was possible, but you did nothing. This is the opposite to feeling your power.

Flex the muscle because there is much further to go...

Small bold actions: lessons learned

When we first started asking people to write new rules, they tended to be big, unwieldy visions of change that were unlikely to result in anything tangible. This is where the idea of a small bold action came from. Here are some tips that might help.

1. Tick off the three golden rules: remember that it needs to be bold, repeatable, and fit within the 9–5.

Do you feel a little nervous? Can you do it more than once? It is part of the work you're already doing?

2. Give it parameters: Once you've come up with an action, get specific. Write down when and where you're going to carry it out, and who else might be involved. It's not uncommon for people's new rules to be 'I'm going to speak up more' but try to pin yourself to a time and date when you're going to raise your hand and ask that question. Otherwise there's every chance it will slip off the radar.

When, where, and with whom will the action take place?

3. Map the consequences: it would be foolish not to, but rather than it making you feel more fearful, this can achieve the opposite effect. The default fear in a workplace setting – I might get fired – is usually a false fear. Sit down, read the policies (if they exist), and quite often you'll find that the small act of disobedience is unlikely to result in a firing and is more likely to result in an awkward confrontation. That, you can handle.

What's the worst possible thing that could happen as a result of this? What is the best possible result?

Chapter Seven

Go to the Edges of the Map

We're not in this to be liked, we're in this to be heard

Tej Samani

Now we come to the heart of the matter. A small rebellion is all well and good, but the real treasure lies out of sight, off the edges of the map, in spaces, conversations, and actions that others daren't touch. Every pirate, historical or modern, knows this.

This is the transition from one or two righteous moments of resistance to a whole new way of thinking and being. Change comes from the fringes, and being a pirate is often about acting in opposition to mainstream practices and opinions. It's not about being controversial for the sake of it, there are good reasons some things aren't popular or don't work, but as the world changes, there's a continual need to shake free of the past and reinvent how we live, work, play, consume, and interact with the planet.

Creativity, innovation, and 'transformation' are what the world wants and needs, but precious little attention is given to what really gets you there. The truth is that you can't reach new territory if you already know it; it requires a willingness to step into the unknown and feel your way through the darkness without being tempted to rely on what feels safe and familiar. Like breaking small rules that are just habits and hangovers, we need to cultivate a willingness to step across boundaries and find inspiration in unusual places.

One brief example from last year showed me both the need and the appetite for this. I was invited into a discussion with a group of students at University College London's School of Pharmacy, led by my friend and occasional collaborator Oksana Pyzik. Oksana is a Senior Teaching Fellow, an expert in global health, and a fierce campaigner against fake medicines. The purpose of the session was to come up with some new ideas for her Fight the Fakes campaign, and she was keen to bring in some fresh thinking and strategies to increase public awareness and engagement around this little known global health threat. How could they be more pirate about it?

The problem is this: 1 in 10 medical products worldwide, from antibiotics to chemotherapy drugs, are fake or of extremely poor quality.[10] They have no health benefit and may even have serious consequences ranging from poisoning, to disability to death. While fake medicines are a global problem, they are more prevalent in countries with weak regulatory systems where it is easier for criminals to slip contraband across state lines. However, trying to understand the extent of this problem and the scope of solutions from a classroom in central London, has its limitations. The Fight the Fakes campaign is global in nature with over 38 partners across the world, but the conventional multi-stakeholder approach which is intended to bring a variety of perspectives to the table, is still limited by members all being on the same side of the law.

This is where it can pay to build some unlikely alliances to try to get closer to the source of the problem. I suggested that instead of having the conversation just with a group of university students studying the same subject, why not open it up to those who can teach you something new about the problem? Invite in some ex-drug dealers, or others who understand the motivations, challenges, and advantages of working within unofficial channels? They would no doubt offer entirely different insights along with a dollop of realism.

10   www.who.int/publications/i/item/study-on-public-health-socioeconomic-impact-substandard-falsified-medical-products-978-92-4-151343-2

Oksana loved the idea, but voiced that she'd be hesitant to take it forward to her head of department. Unbeknownst to the group, the head had slipped into the back of the room, heard the whole discussion and stood up to announce that it was something she'd be happy to try. Seeding this idea felt like a good day's work. It was helpful to have me in the room to put the suggestion forward because sometimes an unconventional idea lands much better when it comes from a fresh voice.

The question then is whether you can run with the radical idea and stick it out through the initial stumbling blocks: the awkward silences, confused expressions and reprimands that may come when you stop adhering to normal patterns. The loneliness that comes when you start to diverge from your peers can be exhausting. Oksana's initial reluctance surfaced because she had grown weary of challenging middle management to take greater risks on creative projects and felt that her maverick reputation was starting to work against her politically. She succumbed to protection mode where in the past she would have been the first to explore unchartered territory.

And she isn't alone. This is the point when most of us would probably hesitate and fall back into something that feels familiar, because all of those uncomfortable feelings send us the signal 'this is wrong'. But ask yourself this question: do you really think it's wrong, or is it just different, and necessary, even? In the long term, staying within limited patterns of thinking and expectations can be more trying than conservative management itself.

If all of this sounds a bit like another way of saying get out of your comfort zone (though that is inevitable), it's intended to go much further. Going to the edges of the map is about a willingness to really engage with the full extent of your imagination – to be more visionary, to turn the world upside down, to consider the opposite of what is usually done. To partner with 'enemies', make mischief with misfits, and be a lot less fucking predictable. Not for the sake of controversy, but because regularly stepping outside of and crossing boundaries can enrich your life in ways you can't imagine until you start doing it. It is about relishing the feeling of being surprised and even shocked, and remembering how much more you have to learn, and realising that is a good thing.

It is also about how to navigate the edges when you get there. How to maintain the integrity of a radical new idea while also making it real? Otherwise it's just dreaming. How and when should you compromise? We've seen just how negatively polarising opinions can affect society, and that is not the point either. Change requires cooperation, and activism as total opposition can fall down very quickly. Pirates enact a delicate duel between what would be ideal, and what can be made real. Sometimes gaining the ground to 'prove' your new model means working in an establishment setting. It is a precarious place to be, but it's what differentiates pirates from mere rabble rousers.

But first, where to find inspiration?

Skewer the skeletons and toast the taboos

A useful way to slip off the edges of the map is to confront the skeletons in your closet. If your team, company or sector has a bad reputation for something that no one is talking about, can you bring it out of the closet and seize it as an opportunity to explore a whole new area in which to innovate? Just by surfacing the one thing no one dares speak, you will surprise people, and surprise is the spirit we want; it is one of the easiest ways to get people to remember you.

In Sam and mine's experience, most organisations barely scrape the surface of the potential for creative thinking because diverse thinking is not really practised or appreciated. Without dipping into any kind of moral argument, suffice to say that teams with a diverse array of life experience, inclusive of more marginal perspectives, have a clearer sense of what is in the closet, and taboo for the mainstream. Therefore, they have lots of rich, untapped content to draw on. For example, most of us are not very comfortable talking about serious illnesses like cancer, let alone talking about it in a way that goes beyond platitudes. But engaging with the subject in a more nuanced way can lead to exciting new endeavours.

In January 2017, a young London-based artist named Sarah Davis was diagnosed with Hodgkin lymphoma. After undergoing the standard chemotherapy treatments, and emerging on the other side, Sarah soon discovered there was one conversation topic that nurses and healthcare professionals did not want to talk about.

'After many rounds of chemo and a stem cell transplant I found myself living in a completely different body. Many after-effects of treatment were made clear to me from the start, whereas others were left completely off the table. Namely, sex – especially sex for pleasure!

'During cancer your body is dismantled. You are slowly put together piece by piece. Afterwards not everything fits the way it used to. I found having sex was uncomfortable and things that gave me pleasure before now caused pain. I cannot fault the support I had regarding fertility but my quest for pain-free sex led to confusion, embarrassment, and disregard. I was angry and knew I couldn't be alone in this.'

It was only when Sarah joined Macmillan's London Cancer Community – an initiative developed by the charity off the back of their 2017 report on cancer inequalities in London 'Mind the Gap'[11] – that she decided to raise the issue of inadequate support around sex and intimacy. After speaking with Sarah, Macmillan Engagement Lead Emma Quintal decided to do some further research and find out whether this was a widespread issue across the community.

'We found substantial evidence around health professionals' reluctance to have these conversations with patients, and similarly, patients not feeling that perhaps their GP or CNS is the right person to ask. We do not expect clinical professionals to be an expert on sexual issues as a result of cancer, but we do expect them, at the very least, to initiate a conversation and signpost to other sources of support if

11 www.macmillan.org.uk/_images/4057%20MAC%20Report%202017_tcm9-319858.pdf

necessary. Unfortunately, women affected by cancer have told us that this is not happening.'

As a result, Emma is now supporting Sarah to tackle the issue by running sex and cancer workshops, but when raising sensitive or taboo issues, it's important to consider how you go about it. Rather than go running headfirst into a deeply personal topic and letting Sarah's experience lead the way, they decided first to host a focus group, 'Let's Talk About Sex & Cancer', providing women with the opportunity to discuss the impact of cancer on their sex lives.

This was done last year in partnership with Sh!, an award-winning female-focused sex shop in Hoxton, East London. The workshop took place inside their shop, recognising that a clinical setting was part of the problem. Macmillan staff attended to support if there were any clinical questions, but really it was a chance for the women to open up, describe their experiences, and explain what would help them. In addition to the lack of advice and signposting from cancer professionals, the focus group highlighted an inability to discuss sex post-cancer with family or friends, or raise it in a public setting (still very much a taboo); that sexual issues were having a serious impact on personal relationships; and that cancer's detrimental impact on body image and confidence due to scarring from surgery has an impact on sex.

Emma said:

'There was a moment when everybody was talking about the physical impact on their bodies – one woman revealed her scar, which in turn led others to... it was a very powerful moment.'

Now that the initial information has been gathered, their aim is to run a programme of sex and cancer workshops with Sh!. Or in the case where a sex shop might be a barrier to attendance, a few of the women have volunteered to host them elsewhere in their own communities. This initial pilot will focus on women with the view to tailor and cater to the needs of different audiences in the future such as LGBTQ+ individuals, and also couples. The workshops will offer practical demonstrations from the Sh! sex shop team, offer the opportunity for women to share their experiences/challenges or tips/solutions and ask the professionals any questions (plus at least one hour socialising session with prosecco and nibbles).

According to Cancer Research 50% of people born after 1960[12] will develop cancer at some point in their lives so there is no good reason whatsoever for this subject to stay in the closet. I met Sarah at an event Macmillan hosted at City Hall marking two years since the beginning of their Cancer Community. The event showcased the stories and solutions that had emerged following a collaboration with ethnographer Dr Adam Gill of Wilding Health. Adam's research uncovered that there were three broad themes accentuating cancer inequalities in London: navigation of the system, emotional support, and language barriers. The event's 'hack session' that I ran with Adam focused discussions on these three areas but with an additional pirate layer. We asked everyone, *How would you take a risk/rewrite the rules or be more pirate to support people to navigate the system and get the right care?*' Sarah's sex and cancer workshops were highlighted as an example.

Lourdes Colclough, Engagement Manager for London said:

'Our London Engagement Team work with seldom heard groups so we constantly need to find creative ways to engage with people falling through the net of cancer care. The sex and cancer project was about tackling taboos and uncomfortable conversations – the workshop was a place where women could meet that was fun and safe with no clinical labels.'

Yet the event did highlight how much their team in London have already internalised a different way of doing things. The conference itself was interspersed with live music and poetry, and at least half of the speakers were members of their cancer communities. They showed a commitment to hear the truth, from the source, regardless of what it might say about how good or bad the system is.

---

12 www.cancerresearchuk.org/health-professional/cancer-statistics-for-the-uk#heading-Three

In giving a voice to seldom heard groups, you find the skeletons, but beyond that, there is treasure.

Plunder your own depths

In many respects, Tej Samani has always been at the edges.

By 15 he had left his third school and concluded that the UK education system did not understand how to help kids like him. Kids who didn't fit into the rigid criteria it set out as academic success, who were frustrated by being forced to learn in one particular way.

Fortunately, Tej was saved by sports. Despite being labelled an underachiever in the classroom, he had always been an overachiever on the court. After leaving that third and final school he became a professional tennis player, triggering a lifelong interest in performance.

What is it that makes people perform really well?
Where does it come from?
What hinders good performance?

He spent a lot of time thinking about these questions but wanted to apply the knowledge to an environment where he saw so much unnecessary wasted potential. Realising that his own life was unusual, the paradoxical experience of total failure at school, combined with extreme success at sport, helped him to see that he could offer something new to the world.

Nine years ago, Tej founded Performance Learning, an organisation that is radically disrupting education. It combines everything Tej knows about performance and teaches kids in an entirely different way: by putting behaviours and aptitudes before knowledge. In much the same way that pirates wrote rules about how to create rules, Tej has created a system that is more about understanding *how* to learn and what makes someone perform well rather than *what* to learn, which can be applied to all areas of life not just traditional academic subjects.

To begin, students undergo a series of online assessments that ask them how they perceive everything from their own ability to their subjects, the teacher, and the environment they are working in. Recognising that school should aim to counter, not compound, low expectations, Performance Learning supports students to change their perceptions and become higher achievers. This is the really interesting part:

'If you have students who are at a D grade, you just need to get them to a C. We do this by showing them how to learn instead of focusing purely on more of what to learn. This is pretty simple, and it doesn't require an in depth understanding of the subject. Once they reach a C grade, they feel differently about who they are as a learner. They start to believe they're not stupid so then you can take them to a B, and then eventually, you teach them how to get an A.'

Using this method, Performance Learning delivers 18 months' worth of school progress in as little as six, thereby closing the achievement gap. In the case of one student, Luke, he was able to move from a predicted E grade at Maths to getting an A in the final exam. For the Maths syllabus he was encouraged to write out the equations he didn't yet 'get' in words, and explain how he felt about them. The purpose of writing the questions down was to detach Luke from his feelings towards the problem, rather than internalising them, which can hinder learning.

'This physiological block is an emotional response that kicks in before our brains have had a chance to take over. It's seeing a hard question and saying you can't do it before you've let yourself try.'

The astonishing result of Tej's method is not just the impact on students' self-esteem, but an 86% accuracy rate in predicting how well a student will perform.

'We are predicting grades solely through how a child feels about a subject. We can predict subject grades up to three years in advance by assessing perceptions via our machine learning algorithm.'

Performance Learning's method presents a serious challenge to the current system, both in how grades are predicted and how students are set according to their supposed ability. PL works specifically with those from gangs and disadvantaged backgrounds, recognising that life experiences have an unrivalled impact on where students see themselves on the ladder of life and their expectations for themselves.

With their help, these expectations can be turned around.

Raise your Jolly Roger

The challenge to stay at the edge of the map is pronounced for Tej because Performance Learning is a method he has to bring directly into schools.

'Up until I read Be More Pirate, I pretty much thought I was running a pirate organisation with Performance Learning, but then I realised that I've been putting off creating certain content because I felt like it would be too disruptive. We were sometimes being misunderstood; for example, one school accused us of bribery because the students who they wrote off as being 'unteachable' ended up achieving the highest results the school ever saw. I'd become afraid of that, but I'd just forgotten that that's where you're supposed to be.

'The book reminded me of why I began this journey but, most importantly, what I went through in school and how I don't want any other student to go through the same. Now we've completely re-branded Performance Learning to speak to our pirate roots and stay true to our crusade.'

As a result of the rebrand they have launched a podcast called *Bad at School* and shifted all the interfaces towards an edgier, student-centred look and feel. Their AI learning platform Plex has been designed to look more like a game than homework, signalling to the audience that this is a very different way of learning, rather than trying to sneak in their approach by appearing more mainstream.

Raising your Jolly Roger, whatever it may look like, to give a much clearer signal about who you are can be a relatively easy way to stake a claim at the edges of the map. Performance Learning has worked with hundreds of schools achieving results in six months that other learning methods can't achieve in 18. The rebrand means giving themselves permission to shout about this – to be braver with their marketing and bolder about the guarantees they can offer.

Developing 'heartware' as well as hard skills

Education is an area where there is huge scope to make radical change. By and large, in Western societies we've been stuck in the same educational models for a very long time and there's a deep need to re-examine what it means to 'educate' and give scope and space to those who are willing to do things differently. On the other side of the globe, one school has actively decided to take a stand and rewrite the rules of what education should be.

Youth Inc in Adelaide, South Australia, are an alternative studio school for young people aged 17–24 who, for whatever reason, have become disengaged from the usual routes into education and employment. Youth Inc take a holistic approach to education, focusing more on developing the whole person rather than passing exams. All the young people still gain formal qualifications but there's a strong emphasis on coaching and mentoring and on what the bigger picture looks like.

Nia Lewis, one of Youth Inc's learning architects, chanced upon a copy of *Be More Pirate* and wrote to Sam in 2018 to get some more copies for an 'Unfucktheworld' hackathon she was planning; an idea that came about while trying to explain the concept of social enterprise to a group of young people.

'I tried all this jargon-filled language to explain that a social enterprise is somewhere between business and charity, and in the end, I was like "guys, it's just a business approach to unfucking the world". Reframing the language really helped, and it was one of the reasons I thought our students would love Be More Pirate. *It's got so much energy. Mischief and meaning is a perfect summary; it's for people who want to create impact but refuse to sacrifice the fun.'*

Seeing how *Be More Pirate* could reinforce the legitimacy of their approach to teaching, Nia then gave another copy to Fred

Heidt, Youth Inc's principal, who also adopted the idea and began to weave pirates into their day-to-day language.

'I loved the pirate reference so much, obviously too much, because some staff and students even snuck into my office and adorned my wall with a Jolly Roger.'

Puns and flags aside, Youth Inc are serious about challenging what it means to 'educate'.

The first principle is a refusal to start people from a point of deficit.

'We deliberately say when they come here "there's nothing wrong with you, there's nothing to fix, you are OK just the way you are." And they're usually quite bewildered.'

Going to the edges of the map can mean giving a voice to that which usually goes unsaid.

The school as a whole is guided by four clear principles – their code, if you like.

1. Be Yourself
2. Be Thoughtful
3. Be Enterprising
4. Be Impactful

This is embedded in the curriculum design, especially Be Yourself, which sounds easy but is difficult to do and unusual to talk about in a school setting. Their principles are brought out in the curriculum framework which aims to develop students in three ways:

- Headware: attitudes and mindset, how you respond and process situations
- Hardware: skills such as creativity, collaboration, and multiple literacies
- Heartware: your identity including values, strengths, experiences, and passion

Lots of schools do work on development skills and mindsets, but very few do the Heartware piece – *who are you and who do you want to become?* Youth Inc have explicit facilitation that helps students to explore values, and how their experiences have impacted who they are.

One exercise they do in order to think about the impact their values have on decision-making is the 'zombie bunker'. Students are presented with the scenario of choosing who gets to stay in their bunker, which has limited supplies, during a zombie apocalypse. They have to choose from a series of character profiles and determine who's in and who's out.

'One team asked if they could break the rules… my reply was yes, but if you do, explain why and how you will rewrite them. They presented a completely different solution in which they chose to save everyone for a shorter time, dividing the rations among more people and explaining how they would spend the time figuring out how they could tap into their unique strengths to survive outside the bunker.'

Model the behaviours you want to see

You'd be hard pressed to find anyone more committed to improving the lives of young people than Nia, but she's keen to emphasise that they don't always get it right.

'We've got a lot of philosophy but we're still learning every day. We fuck up. In the first session I did on identity we were talking about race and sexuality and it was a disaster. It really affirmed some people's identities but left others feeling overwhelmed. So I acknowledged and apologised that it didn't work for everyone and asked for feedback about how we could do this better next time. We were told that some people valued the opportunity to explore and talk to their identities in a 'school' setting, but others were confronted by it because it was so new to them. We've listened to the feedback that not everyone is ready to do this work openly so early on and that in the future it should be opt in, rather than whole group work and that they'd appreciate time to think about it at

home beforehand. We've listened to this and we'll do it very differently next time.'

She points out that modelling is critical to their approach. Rather than just say, 'It's OK to get it wrong,' she demonstrates it. When the Unfucktheworld hackathon didn't succeed as she'd hoped, Nia used it as an example of her own failure, especially since the students had seen her put serious time and effort into the planning.

It's not a stretch to call Youth Inc the first unofficial pirate school. They have experimented with running code camps to help students design their own Pirate Codes, although Fred acknowledges that these have not yet matured and is fine with that. They have no desire to always stick to the plan but instead live day to day with the tension of trying to model the behaviours that represent a pirate approach and resist the pull of the mainstream.

As Fred described it:

'There are these invisible, gravitational normalising forces that operate in a school environment that keep stretching people constantly and you have to find a way to stay at the edges that don't make you sound like a negative whinger all the time. Be More Pirate helps to sustain us, because it's a metaphor and a language that resonates and reminds us.'

Conventional schools are accustomed to doing things in a more navy way, simply because that's what they're used to. The school system has a tendency to want to standardise: to take something that worked at a moment in time with one group of people and make it replicable. There is a temptation to succumb when the system is telling you that this is the right way. Nia said:

'I would walk if Youth Inc started having KPIs, if we started trying to get a certain amount of kids into employment or university. That's not what we're about. Sometimes the young people will have those as their goals, but it's really about creating a life that is meaningful to them as they decide, not us telling them what they should be doing, or what success is. That's the biggest flaw of the education system for me.'

When risk reaps rewards

When positioning yourself against the mainstream, the approach should take into account your level of autonomy and resources. In pirate terms: you can be at the edge of the map and a hundred miles from the nearest country with scarce supplies, or just one mile with a fully stocked ship. The edges of the map exist only because there is a map, so assessing where you are in relation to it matters a great deal. If you fire a cannon will it create a ripple, or a tsunami?

As a tool for navigation, it's worth also saying that maps have always changed over time so should be treated with some scepticism. As a pirate you're ultimately looking to redefine the map entirely, so it's far better and more reliable to navigate using a compass (your code).

In chapter four we introduced you to The Child's Rights International Network (CRIN) and their incredibly detailed and thoughtful Pirate Code. When the team wrote their code to evaluate which work really mattered to them, it took them right to the edges of their sector. The code states:

'If we cannot imagine the world we are claiming to fight for, we will never get there. In a constantly changing world, we need to be creative and adaptive if we are to be effective. While we can be sceptical, it does not mean that we let pragmatism kill ideas and imagination. All change begins with an idea. History is full of examples of small groups of people who came together because they had an idea that then changed the world. You have to find it, explore it and share it.'

From thereon in, they refused to campaign only on the issues that everyone already agrees on (the low hanging fruits of advocacy), but to look beyond, to the things that are barely on our radar, but happen daily.

In their 2018 report, they outline their intention to campaign on the following:

•   The exclusion of children from voting

- The way children participate in the legal system (they mostly can't)
- The bodily integrity of children – including challenging things like virginity testing, routine male circumcision, and the forced sterilisation of children with learning disabilities.

As a result of going to unexplored territory, CRIN's funders have not backed off horrified – quite the opposite. They see them more favourably, because now they're not just one of many NGOs protesting the same thing and trying to prove that they can deliver change more effectively. What they stand for is different and distinct.

At the beginning you may be ignored, shunned, stigmatised or all of the above. Yet so much of what we consider to be 'normal' today was once a peripheral vision. Fly the flag and model your values to draw the attention and admiration of the mainstream, in the hope that the mainstream adapts and, eventually, adopts them.

Prepare for adversity but expect acceptance.

Make time for business to be unusual

Returning to more practical matters.

As you start to interrogate the edges and practise more unusual thinking, it helps to create a regular time and space for it. This has been taken up in one way or another by a number of different teams. The crew at Birds Eye granted everyone 'Fuck It Time' – two hours a week that you would schedule like a usual meeting, but instead it's a meeting with yourself. Two hours during which you can work on any creative project that isn't part of your normal to-do list. By scheduling it, it means you can do it uninterrupted, you protect the time, but you're allowed not to have any particular agenda. The same goes for the marketing team at Sony who began scheduling monthly 'Fuck Shit Up' meetings as a result of their *Be More Pirate* workshop with Sam.

We didn't intend to make all the swearing mandatory, but it does serve a function. First, it grabs people's attention. They're far more likely to remember that meeting than something more run-of-the-mill. Secondly, a bit of shock can break through long established neural connections and shake you out of complacency from the word go. In his book *Intelligent Disobedience* behavioural scientist Ira Chaleff cites the example of an ex-army officer who was pushed to be less obedient by his superior. Whenever the officer felt his captain was issuing an order that didn't make sense, the officer was required to say, "That's BS, Sir".[13] At first, he was deeply uncomfortable with doing so as it directly contradicted his training. But over time, it became an empowering tool that enabled him to feel confident in calling out orders he didn't agree with. Sometimes swearing, or other common, yet irregular language (such as 'pirate') is a quick route to assertiveness.

Scheduling time to think and act differently, to question the rules, to consider the opposites, is critical. One workshop or an annual away day will never be enough to change the behaviour of the team – forget it. You can commit to being pirate in a moment, but really looking at the world in a different light and executing a more pirate way of behaving takes time and practise. For most of us there are years of conditioning in the opposite direction to undo, but it is possible. As we outlined in chapter three, pirates do not have to be natural rebels or extroverts; it's not about showboating or even being the leader. It's more about an ability to let go of preconceived ideas and expectations. It takes practise to live comfortably with our curiosity and the many paradoxes that life presents.

One of the people that Nia gave a copy of *Be More Pirate* to is a young man named Josh Moorhouse. Josh was trained as a jazz pianist and has had a turbulent time over the last few years, both with his mental health and in finding a path to something more

---

13   p.35, Intelligent Disobedience, Chaleff, Ira

meaningful. But, through this, he has learned to embrace being at the edges, and owning it.

'I started feeling these expectations to conform to a standard, to get a "normal" full-time job and earn a "normal" living – whatever that means. But listening to Sam speaking about good trouble and reinventing rules through Be More Pirate was resonating with me so much, until it just clicked. I thought, how many times must I wait to hear someone I respect, or someone I view with authority, say something I've thought before but stayed silent? How many times before I realise I could have been the one to say it in the first place?

'I used to think I was wrong, but what's been significant for me since reading the book, is being able to reframe those moments as not "wrong" or "bad," but as times where I was just following something I intrinsically believed in and perhaps that pissed some people off. I've now been able to find some pride in reframing those moments as rebellion. So, I continue not to turn away from the truths in my adversity, in knowing that moments of fear tell me that this is exactly what I should be doing, and that I need to step into this space to uncover what is waiting to be found – no matter what that may be. Perhaps fear is telling me that I'm close to a discovery, perhaps even a revelation.'

*

The edges are where the future reveals itself, but it is our young people who will have to face that future.

It is apt that much of this chapter highlights the work of people trying to carve out a better experience for the next generation. They will ultimately be the ones who lose or gain from whatever we decide to do or not do today.

If you think the status quo is unlikely to serve them well, then off the map you should go.

Claim the edges: lessons learned

1. Creativity vs Conformity: most companies say they want creativity but when it comes to the culture, often end up rewarding conformity. To overcome the conformity curse and get you to the edges of the map faster, start by asking two questions.

What do we usually do in this situation?

What would be the opposite of that?

Not every opposite answer will provide fruitful new territory, but it's a good exercise to explore possibilities, and do it as a team so that outlandish suggestions, curiosity, and 'what if's' feel more acceptable.

2. Unearth the taboos: be sensitive but curious about the different people, places, ideas, and experiences that you've not yet encountered. Try to uncover some of the less touched on topics, even if they are a bit uncomfortable. It has been very noticeable to Sam and I that so few of the mutinies we see initiated touch on the climate crisis. In comfortable middle-class workplaces, discussing the impact of global warming and how we ought to change business, still seems very much off the edges of map. So ask yourself:

What is not being talked about here, and why?

Who could we invite into this conversation to bring a completely different perspective?

3. Schedule time to fuck shit up: by that we mean create regular time to throw some wildcard ideas in the air and see where they land. Be outlandish and outrageous if it helps unblock some creative damns. You can do this on an individual level too. Simply find time in your diary over the next couple of weeks to do something that both intrigues and scares you in equal measure. The darkness breeds discovery.

Chapter Eight

Build a Crew

Inspired by Be More Pirate, *I keep coming back to mutinies: smaller victories that demonstrate that bigger changes are needed – and how we can organise in a way to make that happen. We will need new allies, so let's inspire them to join us. If a merry band of mutineers target their efforts together, they can demonstrate not just that the status quo should change, but that it can change.*

Nick Martlew, Deputy Executive
Director of Digital Action

Second to the code, nothing was more critical to a pirate captain's success than their crew.

If you left the last chapter thinking that going off the edges of the map might allow for all kinds of crazy, fantastical, and unrealistic thinking, then this is where the crew comes in. Historically speaking, pirate crews were a sophisticated system of accountability and collaboration that managed to honour the collective and the individual simultaneously. That ain't easy to do.

The crew are there not to temper possibility, but to ask sensible questions, to challenge and ultimately improve an idea. Building a crew is not about herding together the same kinds of people, who dress the same and talk about the same things with each other in an echo chamber. Crew building is actually the opposite; it's about problem solving or working towards a goal of some kind, and to fully understand all different facets of a problem you need a wide variety of perspectives, skillsets and life experiences. As per the situation our original pirate heroes found themselves in, it is entirely possible to be united while different, enough to launch a mutiny, rewrite rules and protect what is sacred. This was the first lesson I learned when I began building relationships with everyone in this movement. It opened my eyes to what I was previously missing in having a relatively closed and homogenous personal network.

I also rapidly learned that if you want to get anything done that involves other people, you ought to focus on building the relationships first. This is not the way we usually solve problems – we usually dive straight into the task and hope that the people stuff will sort itself out as we go. Yet anyone who has ever uttered the term 'office politics' will know that all too often, it doesn't. Our connection to each other is our lifeblood but it cannot be manufactured or imported simply by airdropping roles into people's laps. This chapter explores how we can work with others more effectively.

It's become fashionable in the last decade for organisations to refer to their 'community'. However, I'd be very sceptical of any attempts to build real community when it is owned by a central nucleus – be it a brand, a political party or a charity, because the relationship is usually backward. The community ought to be what shapes the organisation, but usually the organisation exerts all its energy on trying to broadcast pre-determined messages to the network. This was ultimately the shift being made by the Mercedes-Benz vans team in chapter five – from customers to community.

Recognising the importance of peer-to-peer connections, and the relationship they have to impact, has entirely changed my perception of what a network or social movement should look like. As one pirate and XR Rebel Anna Hyde put it to me, *When you're in a real community, you just feel it.* Instead of boasting about number of followers or reach, the focus should be ensuring there are strong connections – not between everyone – but between small groups, chapters, or 'crews' within the broader network. These are pockets of activity that will actually get shit done, because information travels much faster along lines of trust. To ensure that these relationships aren't superficial, you have to dive deeper into the sources of individual motivation, points of conflict, and the reasons that might drive people away.

This is not easy or quick work and you might not feel as though you've made enough 'noise' or done any of the other things that a network ought to be doing according to the usual metrics of success, but critical connections are what will have an impact long term.

Whatever your agenda, this chapter is about building a strong crew.

Collaboration – the great lie

Throw the word collaboration or partnerships into a strategy and you're sure to get a few nods of approval in the departmental meeting because, like innovation, it's a universal professional truth that collaboration holds the key to success.

The problem is that we tend to organise ourselves in such a way that authentic collaboration is near impossible. By this I mean that the set-up within most organisations is more geared towards silos than collaboration. The artificial divisions between departments or teams are then reinforced by each one having specific, inflexible targets or KPIs that don't always align towards a shared goal. This wouldn't be such a problem if there was flexibility to change KPIs or goals, but that largely depends on who is setting them, and they often come down from on high to ensure that they meet the wider budget requirements.

So, the first thing that thwarts collaboration is our traditional means of organising ourselves.

Break down silos

Silos are more of a problem when the need for collaboration is critical to achieving your goals, rather than a nice-to-have. Whenever we've worked with employees within local authorities, for example, the biggest issue they cite is a lack of joined up thinking. Despite heroic efforts to the contrary, the set-up means that different aspects of our lives: employment, housing, welfare or social care, are treated as if they exist in isolation from each other.

Of course, departments and job roles provide employees with focus and a way to split workloads so this is not a suggestion that they should be abandoned altogether, just that we ought to make the walls between them more porous. But how?

One pirate who is spearheading a revolution in collaborative online working to create better cross-team communication is Dr Tammy Watchorn, a former employee of NHS Scotland. Tammy is an expert facilitator for something called QUBE – a virtual workspace that comes equipped with project rooms, hackathon, and workshop spaces as well as a range of what they call Performance Enhancement Tools. You login, as you would on any other platform, and appear as a colourful avatar (a bit like a jelly baby) in a space that is modelled on real physical spaces (Sam and I tried it, it was surprisingly fun and quite relaxing). The aim of QUBE is to help a group of people who cannot meet face-to-face, to work together quickly and creatively on complex problems.

Even though it's entirely technology based, Tammy's foray into this new field has been heavily influenced by the way pirates organised.

About four years ago I started trying to gather together others in similar roles to create a sort of underground movement, as we were often fairly isolated across different NHS organisations. It began with leads from different health boards, some were clinicians, some were change managers. Unfortunately, we didn't have a Pirate Code and over time individuals drifted off due to operational work pulling them back, frustrated at the slow pace of change and the never-ending need to constantly challenge the status quo while staying resilient... When I came across Be More Pirate, *it really gave me an understanding of why things didn't work the first time.'*

Tammy realised that she had been trying too hard to lead from the front, so there wasn't really a sense of a collective, or collective ownership. This made it easy for people to drift away. So, she tried again, this time casting the net much wider but letting the group form itself. Everyone else then read the book and shared their thoughts with their own teams. This provided a shared language that everyone understood and that gave them permission to be experimental. The group were all on a similar middle management level so they had the flexibility to do things but weren't so high up the food chain that it would get noticed.

'It worked in part, because people were realising that innovation isn't about shiny gadgets but about people, and how we work and behave. The book gave us insight and ideas into how to make it work. This time it was less about me trying to get loads done, it was more like I trusted them to go back to their own ships and figure it out.'

That is precisely the interesting thing about QUBE. The focus is not really the technology, it's about how to work together effectively. As I write this, we are in the middle of a huge transformation towards remote working because of Covid-19 but so far all we seem to have is Zoom fatigue because we're trying to take exactly what we do in person and replicate it online. Tammy's focus is understanding why that doesn't work and how to rectify it.

She describes digital transformation as having three elements: the digital part (the actual technology), the tools and process (organising), and the culture and leadership (people/behaviours). Up until now, we have pretty much just given people the tech and said 'go', without teaching them anything about how to adapt the rest. You certainly don't get Zoom with a set of suggestions about how to behave, hence we're all intimately familiar with how hideous big video calls can get. A 10-second silence feels like an eternity, prompting someone to jump in unnecessarily and soon it becomes a sequence of quite random thoughts. On QUBE, it's different.

You always write before talking, which gives time to pause and think about the contribution you want to make. Because you're in a virtual space with things to look at (virtual white boards etc), it doesn't feel awkward – or like you don't know what's going on.

QUBE and its jelly baby avatars also strips away levels of hierarchy. In come the surgeon and the nurse and the hospital manager into the slightly surreal environment and you all look the same. This plus the different, more thoughtful, mode of working seems to level the playing field; the idea is to support anyone to write or say what they really think. Unlike video conferencing, QUBE isn't just a space for people to meet, it's specifically equipped with tools to help people problem solve.

'I would love this to be mainstream across the NHS but in some places, it's still seen in the "too novel" category because it's about ways of working and many still want shiny gadgets and old school meetings. Those who do use QUBE (and there are many) are sort of in the pirate camp.'

Unusual it may be, but it's getting results. One case study Tammy highlights comes from a group of 30 senior nurses across Scotland who undertook a virtual leadership programme and now work together on QUBE on a range of activities to improve patient safety. Another project with a team of surgeons saw them develop and test a prototype multi-disciplinary decision-making tool for patients with liver cancer – in just three weeks.

'QUBE has given staff the space (pirate ship) to create their own rules and work collectively and collaboratively. It teaches them new ways of working, leadership, and gives them the confidence to enact and make decisions not only in their peer group but across their organisations. It has been a privilege to work with these teams and I'm amazed not only at what they deliver but how they have grown in confidence and as leaders of real change.'

One team from NHS Health Education England recently won an award at Henley Business School for their work on QUBE. They were tasked with supporting organisational change to improve patient care and health outcomes, tackling a host of barriers such as geographical spread of staff, opposing cultures, legacy loyalties, and differing skill levels. Henley said:

'They have not only been able to open minds and change work behaviours, but reduced travel and increased value-added tasks. They have also successfully created an environment that promotes diversity based on equality. Their work is an example of how the selection and use of available technology can be used to create a culture of learning and progressive change.'

When I spoke to Tammy during the writing of this book, she was flat-out exhausted. The impact of the coronavirus meant the demand for QUBE had shot up. One of the bigger NHS organisations that she's been working with for three years had requested additional 'outdoor' and social spaces now that so many staff are home working; turns out it's the more casual interaction with colleagues they miss most. And it's not just within the UK, Tammy had just begun working with a company in Lombardy, Italy. They wanted new ways to support struggling local businesses.

'Yes, I'm pretty exhausted with the increased workload associated with the world starting to work remotely. But in a good way. Helping find creative solutions to brand new challenges that we have never seen before to help create a new norm, is also really energising.'

Collaborate to share the booty

It is not just the public sector that suffers from collaboration fraud, so to speak. Lots of commercial companies will also *say* that collaboration is a core value but when you speak to staff, the reality is more like competition, and the fallout from that is duplication and burnout. It means lots of people exerting too much energy on the same objective, when they could be pooling resources or money to get the same results. What, for example, would be possible if seven budget holders in an organisation formed a small crew and put just 3% of their annual budget towards one project they all really care about (with or without permission)?

In one workshop we did with a large technology company an idea of this nature arose. The leadership offered an empty statement about the importance of collaborative culture, but when it came to the group work, the sales team admitted that their bonus structure, which pitted each person against the other, meant there was no incentive whatsoever to collaborate. Once they realised they now had permission to imagine something different, they started designing a structure which didn't alter the overall sales target but allowed them to work as a group to achieve it, splitting the profit equally instead of it being weighted towards the highest performer. As a group they recognised that the title 'highest performer' was often bullshit anyway; there were reasons outside of their control why some people could pull in higher sales. The new idea would rectify that and incentivise them to work through barriers together.

Scale for impact not growth

Money should not be ignored in the collaboration equation, no pirate ever would. It might not be the underlying motivation to come together, but it can provide essential glue. In *Be More Pirate* the chapter Reorganise Yourself is all about how to collaborate to achieve scale rather than growth – the obsession with growth being a primary driver of the Climate and Ecological Crisis. So, figuring out ways to be profitable while being collaborative is absolutely vital if we are to have a hope in hell of reinventing our economic models. Or, as I often think about it: *how can you get other people to work for you (so you can stay small) in a way that also benefits them?*

*

For nearly 20 years, Ian Hurst was a typical corporate employee. Every day he would travel into London from his home on the south coast to look after the global insurance for high profile clients like Porsche, Bentley, and Rolls Royce. The work was stressful, but the money was good and enabled him to live a good life: his own home, nice holidays, and meals out etc. Everyone around him assumed that life was fine and dandy.

Then, one day a couple of years ago while he was on a flight back to the UK following an intense work trip, out of nowhere Ian broke down. *'I just started crying. Everyone around me was like, woah. Bless, the woman I was with didn't have a clue. She just said, "chin up mate".'*

Ian soon realised that he was suffering from profound loneliness. Over time, doing work he cared little about, he had become detached from himself and everyone around him. Thankfully, in the weeks after his breakdown, his employers offered time off and support in the form of something called mental health first aid training. This is still quite a new concept in the workplace, but it seeks to recognise that we all ought to be better trained in recognising the signs of poor mental health. Ian was so struck by how effective it was, he soon trained to become an instructor himself and began to reconsider his career options.

Around the same time, he got back in contact with some old friends – Karl Draper-Firth and John Logue – who run a community music and mental health support platform called We Are Hummingbird (WAHB) in their spare time. WAHB encourages people to create and upload playlists and explain what music means to them, at the best and the worst of times. The 12-song playlists published each week are a subtle nod to the statistic that 12 men commit suicide each day.

It was through Karl and John that Ian was introduced to James Scroggs, a Trustee of CALM (Campaign Against Living Miserably) and founder of HOOPMUSIC and MC Overalls. He suggested that if Ian was thinking about leaving the corporate rat race and setting up on his own, he should read a particular book first.

'It was a massive twist of fate really, but that is what my life is all about. On James's recommendation I immediately read Be More Pirate, *and wow. It was so clear that my old workplace was the navy, the establishment.'*

Karl and John offered Ian the opportunity to come on board with WAHB as a full-time director and to incorporate mental health first aid training into the platform under the banner We Are Hummingbird Health. With this came a blank slate and a chance for Ian to chart his own course.

'The first thing I thought about was values. I remember, I was sat in a soft play area of the park with my kids and I thought, this is my chance to write my Pirate Code, that in 10 years' time if we're at a crunch point when someone's flashing money and it doesn't feel ethically right, we'll know what to do.'

His code consisted of five key words spun into a single sentence: We deliver **pragmatic** training that **empowers** individuals to **collaborate fluidly** and **prevent** mental health issues becoming worse.

These words inform how he is approaching all aspects of the business, but there were two things that struck me about how they use collaboration to scale. The first was already in play with the music community side of the platform. All the music content on the site comes from the community. Each week when the latest playlist is published, it's also pushed out to the contributors' personal networks, which can be extensive. Karl and John's connections in the music industry have generated high profile contributions from bands such as The Fratellis and Starsailor. They manage to kill two birds with one stone in simultaneously creating a stream of new content for the site, while also growing the audience (and potential customer base).

The second idea, which came from Ian, was to form strategic partnerships that could build brand awareness. Alongside the playlists (which are free), We Are Hummingbird was already producing and selling merchandise such as t-shirts, hats, and tote bags. When Ian started to think about how they could expand their reach, he decided to approach CALM and offer them £1 of every t-shirt sold in exchange for the use of CALM's logo. This would help WAHB as a new venture to gain legitimacy by being an official partner. Then he approached Music Venue Trust, a charity who have impressive exposure to artists, and offered the same. Through them, he could gain access to and partner with more musicians.

Donating profits to charity is usually only done by big brands seeking to appear philanthropic, not small start-ups.

'My friends were like, why are you giving away money, that doesn't make sense, but the returns have been worth it. I don't think I'd have thought about joining up crews like this, if it wasn't for the book. I was previously in a really cutthroat environment where everyone was in it for themselves but now I look at things differently.'

Being more pirate is a switch from 'who is doing better than me and is therefore my competition?' to 'who is doing better than me and could therefore help me out?'Then figure out what you can offer in return.

Another pirate who has thought carefully about how to reorganise and use more collaborative strategies to turn a profit is James Berg, founder of Picaroons – which he describes not as a company but a 'social media marketing crew founded on pirate principles'. Picaroon is an old word which literally means 'to act as a pirate'. Up until last year, James had spent his career working for big advertising agencies and seen first-hand the paradox of scale.[14] It neither allowed people to do their best work, nor satisfied clients.

In striking out alone, James has built a network of contacts who he can call upon to deliver briefs. He knows their skillsets, their styles, and strengths so that the work can be assigned to the right person. They can deliver on a much bigger range of briefs since no one is bound by hours, role or pay grade. People can opt to take a smaller job that will take a couple of hours or something bigger. This means Picaroons can deliver to any budget but uses the best industry talent, and crucially, the crew are all willing to run against the grain.

'We are building a network of creators who are geniuses at their craft and don't conform to the rules of the establishment.'

14   www.fahrenheit-212.com/boiling-point/the-paradox-of-scale

His model sits somewhere between being part of a team and being a lone freelancer. If you're looking for a freelancer, Picaroons allows you to escape the shopping mall vibe of sites like Fivver but it's more established than informal peer recommendations because there is a unifying story and a standard in the quality of work that James ensures. Everyone who is part of the crew maintains their core independence to do the work they want, when they want. It benefits James to be able to recommend reliable talented people, but critically he avoids the pitfalls and obligations that come with growth.

Know why you're there

Money is all well and good, but no crew is ever watertight without a powerful, intrinsic motivation. Every Golden Age Pirate was motivated at the core by the promise of freedom and a better quality of life. So strong was this desire that they were willing to risk the noose to join a crew. Collaboration works when everyone *really wants to be there*, not because they've been told to be there.

This can happen naturally when the group has had a powerful, shared experience. One of the best examples are NCT groups (National Childbirth Trust). Becoming a parent is a life-changing but often alienating experience, and the people you meet during become lifelong friends. But, crucially, the NCT does not engineer these relationships via any kind of ongoing infrastructure: they don't create online forums or hold meet-ups. New parents stay together of their own accord.

However, organisations who want to 'do collaboration' or facilitate networks, don't always realise that success is more likely if they step back and put official channels to the side, at least for a while. Don't underestimate the power of conspiracy sessions in secret locations for building strong bonds, as this next crew proves.

Kath Smythe is a senior leader at Manchester City Council, and last year she set up a pirate group within.

I'd heard our Chief Exec who's trying to drive a different culture say on a number of different occasions, "You're the senior leaders, you set the culture – if you want change, change, if you want permission, you've got it." I was sitting in a group of really amazing people who do fantastic jobs and thought, what an opportunity, it's up to us to grab hold of this.'

Kath knew that she could kickstart something by being willing to step outside of what they normally do.

'It felt like a risk but I could see that there was nothing about being a pirate that goes against our vision for where we are trying to get to and our values as an organisation, so I decided to go for it. I put up a post on our internal intranet about starting a pirate group. It started with three of us having a brew in a café, talking about how we can make this real.'

This first step of meeting with no pre-determined agenda is really important. Simply talking and sharing; ideally sharing something about yourself that's personal. *What really motivated you to come here?* This builds trust and will be the bedrock of the resilience you'll rely on later down the line.

They then reached out to others they thought might be interested. As the group slowly grew in size, they spent time together working out what really matters to them, what they felt willing to stand up and fight for, and most importantly (because they wanted to make stuff happen) the first rule they were going to break.

'It's really empowering but it felt dead scary at first. We regularly and informally meet as a crew. It was incredible to see how quickly we got into conversations about vulnerability through breaking one small practical rule. The reality is, you're not going to stick your head above the line unless you really care about something, and we found ourselves on a full-on journey that felt really personal working through what is really motivating us here and why does it matter.

'That helped us to connect as a crew and build trust.'

After lots of conversations and a few attempts at rule-breaking, they were ready to build a code.

Here is what the crew came up with:

1. We are motivated by fairness and justice.
We thrive when we are seen, heard, supported, and recognised, not because of our grade or role but because of who we uniquely are and what we uniquely bring.

2. We bring the soul back into our work.
We are committed to breaking the tyranny of emails, rules, and meetings that don't bring value. We will courageously and creatively change how we work to maximise our happiness, effectiveness, and impact.

3. The best ideas come from diverse minds.
We strive to free ourselves from our blinkers and prejudices connecting and collaborating with diversity in all its forms of life experience and expertise.

4. We choose courage and integrity over comfort.
We broach difficult conversations when we see behaviours that are not authentic to what we're trying to achieve.

As they slowly began to put elements of the code into practice, two issues emerged. The first was that other people had become attracted to the group, so there was a question around whether to let the crew grow. There is no right or wrong answer here, it depends on your objectives, but the problem with scale is that you begin to lose critical connections. Author and queen of gatherings Priya Parker's answer to this is to not be afraid of closing doors to keep a meeting meaningful:

'Barack Obama's aunt once told him, "If everyone is family no one is family." It is blood that makes a tribe, a border that makes a nation. The same is true of gatherings. So, here is a corollary to his aunt's saying: If everyone is invited, no one is invited – in the sense of being truly held by the group. By closing the door, you create the room.'[15]

The second issue was when they began to try out article four: courage and integrity over comfort.

'We decided we needed to get comfortable with challenge, and

15   p.38 *The Art of Gathering*, Parker, Priya

work out the places where we're less comfortable, to play and practice challenge.'

They started encouraging the group to have more difficult conversations, but if you don't do it often, it's unlikely you'll be good at it to begin with. Approaching a sensitive subject with tact and respect, while also being direct and as bold as you need to be to, takes practice. Like the army officer in *Intelligent Disobedience* who had to be trained to swear at his superior, don't give up because it feels awkward to begin with. That is one of the benefits of meeting with a crew outside normal hours and formal meeting structures – you can use the space to test out situations, share techniques, and develop your confidence so you're ready for action.

And, while they experimented with trickier areas like practising challenge where the answers will always be nuanced and context dependent, they also seized the opportunity for smaller, repeatable actions or rule breaks that maintain momentum. In line with the second article in their code, at the end of Kath's email signature you'll see the following:

#bemorepirate #breaking the tyranny of emails by:

- Thinking before I email – can I have a conversation instead?
- Taking protected time away from email and spending it focusing on the stuff that will make the biggest difference.
- Checking my tone – am I structuring my email in a way that I'd be pleased to receive?
- If it's bad news, I won't deliver it by email.

Seek out the ear of the enemy

As Kath's crew discovered, you cannot hope to build a strong organisational culture where people are able to collaborate effectively if you ignore or gloss over issues that bring about resistance and conflict. As I said at the beginning, ignoring politics, or assuming that you're all on the same page about a particular issue can seriously derail projects, instead it can be beneficial to invite in the resistance and make it a deliberate focus.

This is what Barry Verdin did when he found himself leading a project that had the potential to be transformative but was at risk of being done in a one-dimensional way. Barry is a business change specialist at the Open University. The title might give it away, but his purpose is to try to manage big change programmes and understand, ahead of time, all the factors that might undermine success.

'I've always been the maverick in my team, perhaps sometimes less constructively, but Be More Pirate *has helped me to focus and harness that energy in a more positive way.'*

This project was the kind that a lot of us will have seen in the last decade or so. The university was looking to upgrade the software that sends out all their email communication because the current system was both non-compliant from a GDPR perspective and inaccurate. Having been part of a project like this myself, I feel Barry's pain. When you have marketers, faculty, and technical staff all coming from a different perspective, there is usually conflict around scope, ambition, and necessities versus nice-to-haves. It is an almighty challenge to unite everyone behind a shared vision of what 'good' looks like.

The first temptation was to implement a tactical solution and simply stick with an upgraded version of what they already had. And what they had, in Barry's opinion, was not great. All emails were sent out as long messages in plain text without images. There was no personalisation. The Open University has more learners in Scotland and Wales than any other university in the UK but there was rarely a regional voice in the communications they sent out. Here was a chance to rectify that and redesign the process so that they could maximise the impact of communications with some basic standardisation around branding and quality.

What Barry needed was for everyone to understand the

potential benefits, while appreciating each other's point of view. He wanted the faculty to see that marketing wasn't a dirty word and could really benefit them.

'I feared we would do the usual thing of building something and then discovering the resistance.

'Rather than go head to head with the resisters I invited them in. I created a "challenge group". I told them I wanted to listen and that I needed their feedback early on in the project so we could design it to help them from the outset. There was some scepticism. They didn't trust me.'

Nor did Barry's superiors. In fact, he was expressly forbidden from taking it in this direction. The project sponsor was really uncomfortable with the idea, fearing delays and scope creep, but Barry pushed on and kept emphasising the risk of not doing this and in the end decided to go ahead anyway.

Initially, he sought out the individuals he wanted to be involved and spoke to them one on one (building critical connections), explaining his idea and asking whether they'd be interested in becoming part of the project group. Then he scheduled the first clandestine meeting to bring them together.

'There was no precedent for doing this – we have advisory groups, but they've never been instructed to challenge and be pirates. I asked them to tell me all their concerns because it really needs to be flushed out at the beginning. But it was the most energising and positive project meeting I can recall. We had such productive feedback that we could change our design briefs before the project had even initiated.'

One significant point of conflict and discussion was the roll out. Do they go with a big bang, or try smaller pilots under the radar? They separated into different groups to understand the different perspectives on this. By the second session, Barry told the project sponsor what was happening and gained permission to carry on with this approach, which prompted her to ask if she could come in and chair the sessions. Sticking to his pirate principles, he pushed back, fearing this would formalise it and constrain how people expressed their views. The project has since continued to go from strength to strength.

'*We collectively gained a greater appreciation of different perspectives and the negativity was swept aside. We now have a project which is truly stakeholder led and I have real confidence in delivering success. We have managed a massive project risk and turned it into an opportunity. We have set a new standard that I expect to see being used more widely across the organisation in the future. And I had so much more fun doing it.*'

If you refuse to bury it, you can make resistance valuable and even a compelling reason to become involved with a project. However, it's worth saying that in this story everyone involved had a vested interest in the long-term success of the project, so there was clear reason for cooperation. It would be far more frustrating to try to partner with a group or individuals who were vehemently opposed to your proposals. As always, seeking out the ear of the 'enemy' is a suggestion and not a hard and fast rule.

When mutinies become movements

Getting it right as a small group is the first step, but now we move into looking at how a small, purposeful group can evolve into something bigger.

For Sam and me this next story might be the most satisfying of all. Why? Well firstly because, pirate jokes aside, we have managed to find the *real* Pirates of the Caribbean to replace Disney's bastardised version. On Turks and Caicos, a small crew of 'climate pirates' have emerged, instigated by marine biologist and coral reef specialist Franziska Elmer who felt it was important to get her students involved with combatting the climate crisis. The students agreed and Climate Pirates were born.

Secondly, it is beautifully circular. When I first spoke to Franziska and asked her what it was about *Be More Pirate* that made her pay attention, she said this:

'*I loved all the stories of people who started something small and then it became big. The examples are the really cool parts.*'

Now she has become one of those stories.

Originally from Switzerland, Franziska has been based in the Caribbean for the past three years teaching students about marine ecosystems, alongside undertaking a research and development project on how macro algae can generate energy on a large scale (which I'm told, has huge potential for climate change). Working day in day out with marine life she was of course concerned about environmental issues, but as the global climate change narrative took a turn for the apocalyptic she really began to pay attention.

'Suddenly it switched from OK, no one's really doing anything to what will you tell your kids or your grandkids – are you going to act? It became a lot more serious. I was reading Be More Pirate *at the same time and when it came to the question. "What is worth fighting for?"... I thought, this. The climate crisis.'*

The first thing Franziska did was to change her usual climate change lecture. Until then, the lecture was very scientific and peppered with graphs about ocean acidification and temperatures etc. Which is fine, but it did not have the impact on the students that was needed. So she decided to switch it up.

'I purposefully shocked them by first explaining that if we surpass 1.5 degrees, we'll lose our coral reefs. I then asked, "Who wants to be a coral reef scientist?" A lot of them do – it's why they're there. I then said, OK, if that's what you want, let's see how long you have to make your career, and I showed them the climate clock website that has a clock ticking down from 12 years, which is how long we have to turn things around according to the IPCC report.'

That hit home.

She's now including more information about the social science side of climate change such as the concept of greenwashing and how advertising persuades us that green products will compensate for non-green products, rather than highlighting the bigger truth that we need to start buying less altogether. Or, how we focus lots of attention on a single issue to feel like we're doing something positive, all the while ignoring the areas where we're still contributing heavily to carbon emissions.

Such as flying halfway around the world to a conference.

This was a personal bugbear of Franziska's. Every four years the International Coral Reef Society holds a conference for 2–3000 coral reef scientists to come together in one place. This year it was due to be in Bremen, Germany, in July (now postponed until 2021). At the end of the conference, a big consensus statement is made by leading scientists with an appeal to help save the corals through unprecedented, rapid change. And yet nothing is said about the fact that they all fly to be there.

'To me it doesn't make sense. How can you ask leaders to make big changes, if you aren't doing it too?'

Her small bold action

One day Franziska decided to raise this by speaking out on the coral science community email Listserv which has about 5,000 recipients.

'The young people are going on strike, yet it's our job to protect the planet. What are we doing? It was my first time posting on that email list and it completely exploded.'

Someone of course brought up the fact that flights are offset, but Franziska pointed out that this was merely making it neutral – shouldn't they be thinking much bigger about what they could do as a community? Plan actions alongside the conference that will draw attention and shake up people?

As a result of the challenge she posed on the Listserv, Fran made an ally and new friend, Judy, who has researched reefs in the Caribbean for decades. A few months later, a new voice appeared on the Listserv: Chelsie, a researcher based in Hawaii. Chelsie didn't want to fly to the Bremen conference either, but instead wanted a related event remotely from Hawaii. She'd emailed the conference organisers to ask if it would be possible to run a local event in tandem, but they didn't respond. Fran and Judy, however, thought this was a great idea.

'We thought, perhaps we and our colleagues could do something remote too from a location in the Caribbean.'

They were inundated with regional responses to the idea, however, it's still expensive and difficult to fly around the Caribbean so the event has now escalated to multiple locations. After putting the word out to others in the wider network, there are now 16 hubs around the world who plan to put on a local event in the week that the large Coral Reef conference was supposed to be held in Bremen, including people in locations in Cuba and Venezuela who rarely are able to attend the main event.

New rules: slow conferencing?

It's down to each hub organiser where and how they want to do it, because it's really for their community. But the general idea is to make it an educational event about corals and the climate for both scientists and the wider community – inviting in school and university students and people from the environmental sector. The plan was to host plenary talks by Caribbean-based scientists including live virtual Q&As, run workshops, and they were planning to show the plenary talks from speakers at the main coral reef conference in Bremen until it was postponed.

The hub events are still going ahead and will have happened by the time this book is published. The fact that bigger events are cancelled may work to their advantage. The flexibility that small, local, online events offer is a real win during this pandemic. They also expanded their virtual reach, by opening up a YouTube channel for local talks by any coral reef scientist or practitioner since many scientists will have research they now can't present anywhere.

This is part of their plan to try what you might call 'slow conferencing' by asking researchers to upload their talks as videos then allow a couple of weeks for the community to watch them and ask questions to the video makers. They're taking inspiration from Ken Hiltner at USCB[16] who has written about doing

16   hiltner.english.ucsb.edu/index.php/ncnc-guide

conferences this way and suggested that it gets three times as much engagement.

In making it up as they go along, Fran and crew are finding new and interesting solutions. At the time of writing, 85 researchers have expressed intent to upload a video, and 566 people in Brazil alone are interested in following the programme. Even though the July events will be mainly virtual, it felt important to do *something* rather than cancel everything, since climate change is definitely not cancelled.

Initially, Franziska's crew got into a bit of (good) trouble with the executive director of the ICRS because they'd begun promoting their events as remote ICRS meetings. With a hint of a threat, they were told categorically they couldn't do that. However, after some dialogue, the ICRS agreed to a potential collaboration for the next event.

'We don't want them to hate us, we want to show them that our event works.'

In striking the right balance between necessary challenge to those who set the rules, and a degree of cooperation, you can prove that your way should be the new way. It is the ultimate pirate measure of success: when others start following your new rules.

A good idea will spread, and it's OK for people to take it and make it their own. Fran's story mirrors the way *Be More Pirate* has moved from one book into a movement. As you can see from this chapter, our crew is really more of a fleet, comprised of lots of individual pirate ships each with their own interpretations of what matters and what battles they can fight. Those crews should feel empowered to go at it alone, with the back up of the wider network. My job, as I see it, has been to build relationships with the captains, because when the time comes to act, relationships will be the foundation of success.

The artistic mutiny

Another of those pirate captains is Yorkshire-based producer Sarah Shead. She has spent the last 10 years running a business that helps artists to navigate the arts sector by attracting funding and support for their projects.

Independent artists make up over half of the entire UK arts sector, but they often struggle to keep their head above water because of a disproportionate amount of funding going into buildings and organisations. Partly it's a result of historical hierarchies and smaller outfits being perceived as risky in comparison with traditional norms, and partly it's the way the system doles out the dollar.

Sarah first began questioning the efficacy of the system years ago, while working in a middle management role at an arts organisation that received over a quarter of a million pounds of public funding each year.

'It struck me that there was all this funding pouring through the rafters but absolutely none of it is going to the artists we were supposed to be supporting.'

By the time staff overheads and facilities had been accounted for, Sarah's actual budget to support artists was zero. Maternity leave gave her the chance to think more about the problem, and she started exploring whether she could help funding reach them directly. After a couple of successes, she was pulled further into requests for ongoing support, and by the end of her leave she had carved out a whole new job for herself. That job became a company: Spin Arts, which has now been going for close to 10 years. Sarah and her colleague Rosie Watt fill the gap she originally identified: how to get money directly to independent artists.

But last year, she began to feel uncomfortable again.

'I knew I'd learned how to navigate the sector really well. I could teach artists how to jump through hoops to get the funding they needed. But I increasingly feel I'm still doing them a disservice because fundamentally the system is broken. How can we expect society to value

arts and culture, if the sector itself isn't investing in, valuing, and taking care of the artists and independents that make it? So, I started to think it was time to challenge the whole system and put my head above the parapet.'

Sarah came across *Be More Pirate* after hearing Sam on the *Reasons to be Cheerful* podcast, and very quickly saw parallels between how pirates organised and the way she had been running her business. One evening, she took five of her collaborators back to her house for dinner. Over food and wine, Sarah raised some of what she'd been reading in *Be More Pirate* and the idea of a pirate crew within the cultural sector to challenge hierarchies and the way resources are distributed, really excited everyone. The next day Sarah set up a Facebook group to house the idea.

'This was on Thursday. On Saturday I woke up and saw there were 95 people in the group. I thought, "fuck!"'

'It definitely wasn't strategic…'

A month later 400 people had joined. Now there's over 1,000, and Sarah has officially named it an Artistic Mutiny.

Transparency and turning the other way

Realising that she'd galvanised everyone but with no idea what to do next, she began by sharing some provocations to start a conversation and initiate action. One of Sarah's most protracted frustrations with arts funding and the organisations it is often invested in, is a lack of transparency. As the newly appointed captain of this crew, she felt the best way to challenge the behaviours she disliked was to model ones she did like. So, she decided to openly share her own day rate and start a debate about what it meant and why she felt it was justified.

'But how did the girl from a working-class, single-parent background, with a shoddy education, who started out aspiring to work in Topshop (because she didn't think she was clever enough to work on a bank cashier), get to the point where she thought she was worth £300 per day?'

This post generated a healthy argument about what it means to be valued in the arts, but Sarah's point is this:

'I don't see this mutiny being about any of us making a better case to be paid more in our current system. That simply isn't going to happen. The case we have to make is for a new system. I am up for that…100%, but little old me storming in there isn't going to change it. Thousands of us making a noise might. The fight is starting small for now, but I'm not playing around at this and I absolutely need every dancer, actor, musician etc., independents, and passionate people in organisations to stand by my side, united as a group and loudly ask for the same thing.'

By the end of last year, Sarah made the decision to go down to three days a week with her former business and take two days to focus on working with this new crew to make it happen.

Then came coronavirus.

As the health crisis kicked off an economic crisis, the self-employed of course found themselves in an even more precarious position than usual. The Arts Council acted swiftly but their response reallocated a lot of the funding that *would* have gone to independents, towards organisations. In retaliation, a petition was created to express the upset. Within days it had 500+ signatures and was circulated around Sarah's crew.

And yet, she didn't sign. Although this might seem like the opportune moment to mobilise her network, she didn't. Something stopped her.

When everybody looks one way, pirates look the other. Rather than running headfirst at the most likely target, a pirate sees the long game and picks their battles to protect the crew. This is when you know you've really become a pirate, when you're no longer predictable. When you've stopped looking to the outside world for direction, but have spent enough time running riot with your own imagination and instincts and are paying more attention to what's possible, not what's probable. The captain has to not only trust the crew but trust themselves.

So, Sarah chose a different response. She wrote a love letter to the Arts Council and an explanation about her actions to the crew. I have included a shortened version of this below. It is, in my opinion, an example of the kind of transparency and leadership needed.

I NEED TO UNDERSTAND WHY – A LOVE LETTER TO ACE

I've written a fair few posts over the past few months about the injustices we see in the Arts. This one feels a bit risky, a bit out of kilt with my first instinct, but considering all my work evaporated overnight, there's really nothing to lose.

Like most people, Arts Council England's announcement about their emergency response to Covid-19 was one of mixed emotions. Upon first glance I thought 'good on them' for turning this around so quickly, but it didn't take long until the realities of it started to unravel (project grants among others being suspended for the time being). Many of our lifelines snatched away before our eyes.

My first instinct was to email them, write a letter laying out every detail of how devastating this was, petitioning and protesting. I realised that I was experiencing fear, grief, rejection... but instead I could choose love. I do love the Arts Council. Without them my life simply wouldn't have taken the path it has, and when I read their 10-year strategy earlier this year I loved them even more because it made me feel like more people in this country were going to experience what I had.

What if I don't kick and scream that it feels unfair?

What if I don't position myself in opposition to all of the organisations who will be thrown a longer lifeline through the emergency funds?

What if the world as we knew it has changed forever and the systems that used to work for us won't work in the months/years ahead?

I'm worried that the public anger and upset we all have may do them more harm than good, and in turn more harm to us and the communities we reach.

I question my thinking around this too. In many ways being a pirate makes me think of battle, of activism, of fight for change. I know that energy feels more productive, but as I spend more time indulging in this daily pirate practice I realise that 99% of the time it isn't that, because 99% of the time pirates were not in battle. Being a Pirate is about Transparency, Accountability, Democracy, Diversity, Equity, Fairness... and so much more.

Do ACE's decisions feel fair? No.

Do I want to give them a piece of my mind? Yes.

Can I see the view from their ship? No.

Do I have a lot of unanswered questions? Yes.

Have I asked all the questions I need to? No.

My pirate tactic is this:

I have written to ACE and asked them that if I collate the questions independents have, will someone take the time to respond and help us understand the battle they are fighting.

These conversations might be really uncomfortable. The process may expose that their decisions were stupid and poorly considered. We may all still feel just as angry and upset as we do now, but at least we'll have the full picture. Only then can we assess their strengths and weaknesses and go into battle being more prepared than we currently are.

This tactic won't be for everyone. You are well within your right to disagree with me because everyone's voice is welcome here.

Keep up all that you are doing. You are all inspirational.

I'll let you know of any progress that comes from this.

Sending love and solidarity to all x

Sarah received a response back from the CEO of the Arts Council England which helped her to understand the picture more clearly, although truthfully it didn't have the substance she was looking for. She wrote back to say that she respectfully disagreed but understood that perhaps now was not the right time to deal with all her questions.

'I feel like the mission we have is much bigger than just this moment. I don't have the answers now, but I'm convinced that I have the networks to work it out.'

The conversations continue and the networks are active in holding their stakeholders and industry bodies accountable for their decisions and actions. Sarah is demonstrating an ability to lead *and* share power. To challenge and be challenged back. To think independently *and* hold space for a large number of people to feel united behind something. Embracing apparent contradictions and accepting that they will live side by side is the only way to get through periods of uncertainty, and a vital skill to be honed by any pirate.

Reorganise to redistribute power (officially)

We're now near the end of crew building territory, and I want to leave with a proposition.

What might it look like if we were to go beyond informal crews, small mutinies, and mass protest movements? What if we were to truly reorganise society according to fairer, more democratic, economic, and social models, so that official bodies more closely resembled the structure of pirate crews? Is this some kind of crack-pipe dream exhaled over a two-page *Guardian* spread? Sometimes it is, yes. But in this next case, no.

In Coalville, an ex-mining town in the East Midlands with a population of about 35,000, a small crew have set up an organisation called TH!NK FC that aims to radically reorganise and redistribute the power. Inspired by a blend of Co-operative Principles, Asset Based Community Development (ABCD), and *Be More Pirate*, it has one goal: to level the playing field.

TH!NK FC was founded by Deana Wildgoose – a woman with deep knowledge of her community and an all-round force to be reckoned with. When she was suddenly made redundant from the heritage, community, and youth charity she'd been with for over two decades, she decided to take everything she'd learned and build a new ship, bringing on board social enterprise advisor Ian Wilson. It was Ian who introduced her to something very few people have heard: a C.B.S.

In legal terms a C.B.S, otherwise known as Community Benefit Society, is about as pirate an organisation as you can get today. It's similar to a co-operative, with a few more bells and whistles. It is fully democratic and owned by the members; anyone who supports its values can be a member and everyone has one vote, irrespective of the amount invested. It's also an investment vehicle, somewhere you can put your money (through a share offer or loan), knowing that it's being put to great social use. For your share you can earn interest depending on the rules the members set, and you can get your investment back once the C.B.S is up and running and sustainably trading. If you have ever heard of a community shop or pub then these will most likely have used a C.B.S to do it. A C.B.S can also have charitable tax status, giving it similar tax advantages to a charity without being one and making it eligible for most grants and social investment programmes. All of its assets can be locked into its structure; profits don't accumulate to one landlord or faceless shareholders, but to the community.

That's a lot of info, so why does any of this matter? Ian put it this way:

'The problem is that people don't have the agency and control they need over local assets or decisions; they are not used to exercising their democratic muscles, and are often defined by their "labels", rather than given tools and opportunities to define their own solution from a place of strength. That is what we are wanting to challenge and change at TH!NK FC and in Coalville.'

ABCD is part of their approach because it positions people as the solution to social and economic problems in their communities, not just burdens on the state. By the time this book is out, Deana, Ian, and Victoria at TH!NK FC, plus a group of local individuals, will become the founding members of a new C.B.S. in Coalville: Coalville C.A.N (communities and neighbours). TH!NK FC's role will be as a catalyst and connector to help get it up and running, and to create and share the toolkit with other groups who might want to do something similar.

Already they have identified buildings which could be owned and used by the community through the C.B.S. An old bank in the centre of a half empty shopping centre which could be transformed into The Bank of Ideas; The Rex – an iconic art deco cinema, a recently closed Central England Co-operative Superstore, a much loved empty Co-operative Department Store, and a Council 'owned' Market. All of which have been or are about to be shut down and (at time of writing) there are no plans in place to use them for anything else.

Their plan is not without its challenges. A lack of ideas and ambition from those in the position of power; silo thinking in large organisations; lack of belief in the possibility of change in the community; inflexible planning rules that don't have a category for 'flexible creative, enterprise and community space'; land banking development companies; and not so discretionary, discretionary business rate relief to name a few. But Deana and Ian are meeting them head on, involving others, negotiating and jumping through hoops, being patient while the bureaucratic machines move slowly. It's painful, uncertain, and unpaid; issues that on their own could put off even the most determined of pirates.

However, the alternative is to continue with the way things are. If we don't attempt to disrupt today's 'common sense', then that Co-operative site will remain empty while a deal and planning is negotiated with a developer. The end result will be 20–40 new houses (probably not affordable and definitely not eco-friendly) and one tidy profit for the developer. The market will be closed, taxpayers' money will be spent keeping it closed, and eventually it will be taken down or it will fall into disrepair.

'What if we can imagine something different? What if the market could become a multi-purpose youth and event space, creating hundreds of local opportunities for people to connect, earn, and play? What if the Co-operative Superstore could become an urban sport and community facility with people from the local and wider community delivering activities that they want? What if there was a learning centre at its heart – a space to explore the School of the Future, one with relevance, underpinned by collaboration and enterprise? There is room for it all. There are funds to help make it possible. There is a vehicle, a C.B.S., to manage it. What's incredible – and obvious to communities – is the energy, the people and the passion are right there in the community. In just a few days of mentioning some of these opportunities, TH!NK FC have met enough people with ideas sufficient to fill the

19 football pitch-size Amazon fulfilment warehouse that's recently opened nearby.'

It is in small towns like Coalville that the choice becomes clear. It's time for everyone in a position of power to stop hiding behind platitudes about systemic complexity. Though TH!NK FC might sound like a small initiative without proof of impact yet these ideas represent the possibility of a new social contract where people can have ownership over things affecting them, alleviating the burden on the state and reducing the risk of big business exploiting the gap.

As the climate crisis grows darker and social inequality is showing no signs of backtracking, we need a different way to organise ourselves at a national and international level. Millions are spent each year on management positions in public services and yet these roles, even if they are said to be asset based or innovation focused, have not stemmed the tide of inequality. Neither have charities or social enterprises successfully changed the status quo at a systemic level, perhaps because neither are truly collaborative; they still rely on transactional relationships between citizens and organisations. The charity or enterprise 'does' and the people 'receive', when what we need is active participation, genuine ownership, and pirate thinking.

Rather than speaking about the left-behind towns and the supposedly left-behind people as if they are entrails dragging behind the bigger cities – relics with no possibility, no imagination, and no spirit, much more could be done to understand and support the efforts of leaders like Deana and Ian whose real strength is their ability to build and maintain relationships. It's not just Coalville either. I've seen evidence of heroic efforts to build crews in places like Chesterfield, Swindon, and Mansfield, but all too often the captains risk becoming exhausted and demotivated before the real impact can happen because the support is not there.

So, if 'be more entrepreneurial' was a mantra for the last few decades when we were hopeful that technology or a single genius might save the day, then 'be more pirate' is what we will need in the decades to come. As the likelihood of conflict over land and resources increases, we must reorganise ourselves in a way that really does redistribute power and put a little more faith in the people who are out there connecting people, trusting that if the intention is good, they'll work it out as they go. The bigger risk is that we don't try at all.

The definition of resilience in the twenty-first century is about how we choose to work together.

Building a crew: lessons learned

1. How you gather matters: if you're forming a new crew, pay attention to when and where you meet. Start with no agenda, the first objective is to get to know each other, sharing your experiences and values will become the bedrock of action. It won't happen if the meeting is officiated, well, like a normal meeting. Meet in informal or inspiring settings. Create a different kind of atmosphere that allows people to let their guard down. And think about whether you need to put a limit on the amount of people in the crew to ensure the connections between existing members don't become diluted. What you're looking for is some real buy in, not easy come, easy go.

2. Create a shared language: whether it's a code of behaviour, using the language of pirates or a shared vision statement. Arriving at something that binds you together is a consistent feature of every crew.

3. Make action simple, to begin: collaboration falls at the first hurdle because we are too ambitious about how much can be achieved while we're being pulled in different directions by competing priorities. Try instead a kind of tit-for-tat partnership to establish trust. *Work out three things you can offer and three things you want.* Agree to swap one each with another person, team or organisation. I'll put you in touch with xxx, if you give me advice on x,y,z – the goal is just to fulfil an obligation to each other and create a baseline for future work.

4. Use the crew as a sounding board: the main advantage of having a diverse group is not that they are an echo chamber of unwavering support, but a sounding board offering sensible challenge. You need a crew that shares your values, but not necessarily your view (point). Don't exclude those with a conflict of opinion; try to invite in the challenge and ask questions to understand why it has arisen. Transparency in your opinions and decision-making will make any subsequent actions stronger as a result.

5. Share power: all our crews have found ways of working together more equitably. This is not the same as having no roles, responsibilities or leaders, it simply means that the structure you have includes and enables, rather than subjugates or controls. It might be that you find ways to work together to pool resources or skills and split profits as James and Ian did, or you steal power from the navy and devolve it to others, as Franziska, Sarah, and others are doing. Crews bring power back to more people.

6. Practise being pirate: having a crew is an opportunity to test your pirate ideas. Practise the uncomfortable conversation topics on the people you trust – talk through real-life scenarios, write out the email you REALLY want to send and show it to the crew. Then when the time comes to act, you will have the confidence of acting from experience, not impulse.

It isn't Pirate to Seek Permission

Because if we had just one hour in your sun
We'd show you how it's done
We'd show you how quickly things can turn around
Go on, give us one hour in your sun
And watch us bloom a field of colour
Look, how we flourish with no sun, no heat or warmth
Because we know how to make love grow in the frost
In the hard dirt, in the winter underground
We make magic mushroom from shit
And spin gold from flakes of hard life
Our hunger it bears, our thirst we share
No boots, no armour, nothing but love drives this
And love is where this comes from and
Love is who this is for and love knows
We have nothing but each other to protect this
No gloves, bare hands, no certainties
And no money, no, never any money
So go on, I dare you, and I dare it
Give us a go on your sun and watch how we'd share it
Give us a paddle in your sunlight, a splash of shiny-shiny
One hour of the sun that is fixed on you and your privilege
For look how strong we are and how tall we can already stand
Without your sun, without your gold and
Without your permission.

– *Salena Godden*

Chapter Nine

Re-humanise the System

It's not the workforce's fault but we have gotten into such a mess where everyone just replicates the same structures and approaches at a rapid rate. It's a pandemic of scale and spread. The transactional drowns out the relational and meaningful – but it doesn't work for complex human issues.

Naomi Davies

This chapter was the hardest to write, and yet it may be the most important one of all.

What was it that the pirates were doing when they challenged the navy? When they created their own rules to live by? What were they saying was really wrong here?

It seems to me that they were saying this: we are not cattle, we are people. We have rights, we have names, dreams, and desires. We have minds that hold endless potential, and so long as we're bound like cattle, we'll fight for freedom.

Pirates emerge when there is unfulfilled potential; when a system attempts to restrict and homogenise us. When it forces us to respond in a way that does not do justice to who we are. To be more pirate, is to also, somehow, to be more human. More human, less robotic, less box ticking, less computer says no. Less turning away from suffering.

There was a fundamental honesty about the Golden Age Pirates that was both wicked and wonderful. They designed their codes not with utopian ideals but with realistic optimism. The pirates' creative rebellion that began with a few individuals and ended with a proto-democratic republic on the island of Nassau, was an ability to see through the system. They shone a light on the fact that rules are only made up constructs created by flawed people, at a moment in time. They are not infallible. All rules can be reconsidered. No idea should be beyond scrutiny.

Pirates were criminalised not because they were violent (as we are led to believe), but because they refused to play by the *specific rules of violence* set out by the group of people who had amassed enough wealth to be the ones who decided. And as the world was carved up according to coin, pirates did not play by the rules of the map set out by the establishment either. When a pirate captain named Benjamin Hornigold refused to plunder English vessels because he retained an attachment to his nationality, his crew deposed him from command. All pirates were required to abandon their home nation, and, in essence, commit instead to a shared humanity – to principles that *anybody* could opt into.

To be more pirate is to be more human because it means looking at what is going on around you and coming to your own conclusions about what matters and what doesn't. It is about a quest towards your own original, not inherited, thinking. Thinking as much with your heart, as with your head.

Gradually, and sometimes very subtly, we have replaced the vital human elements in our work and personal lives, with processes, machines and screens – and used them as shields behind which we hide from the stickiness but miss the wonder. The 2020 global pandemic of Covid-19 during which this book was written, turned those screens into very real shields, and yet, connection to each other and our innate human qualities also became the vaccine we didn't yet have.

The question now is: will we hang on to what we think matters and will we re-humanise the systems that risk forgetting?

People over process

The outbreak of coronavirus highlighted the cracks in healthcare systems across the world. In the UK, we clapped on our doorsteps to show gratitude to our National Health Service – knowing that it has been underfunded for years and is full of dedicated but largely exhausted employees who will go above and beyond despite often feeling overlooked and undervalued.

It was certainly a surprise to Sam at first that the sector where *Be More Pirate* has gained the most traction turned out to be health and social care. The book (he thought) spoke more to the millennial generation, since it was written with the young entrepreneurs he'd always worked with in mind. But pirates are truly born out of hierarchical environments imbued with lots of rules and high levels of risk. Some of those rules are regulations and therefore essential, but some are outdated, overbearing, and unhelpful. In a bid to outrun the cracks over the last few decades, we've seen an efficiency echo chamber emerge – one which often prioritises outputs, data, and middle management (under the guise of increased productivity) over empathy, compassion, and human need, meaning that, in pirate terms, our NHS can feel a bit like the navy of old.

In response to this, a different group of pirates surfaced: older and more experienced, but equally hungry to put their deep knowledge to better use in order to protect and improve a system that is precious. The vast majority of this chapter is therefore devoted to a crew who we generally refer to as the 'health and social care pirates'. They are an ever-growing coalition of professionals spread across the system, the majority of whom live and work in Greater Manchester. 'Re-humanise the system' is really their war cry.

It began with two women who regularly remind me of a modern-day Anne Bonny and Mary Read – so committed are they to piracy. Cat Duncan-Rees and Naomi Davies were among the 10 people to stand up and speak at our first event on the *Golden*

Hinde and announce their intention to start a crew. Naomi is a former mental health nurse of 20 plus years, who now works for the innovation foundation, Nesta.

I start with Naomi's story to emphasise that the criticisms of the system, ultimately come from a place of love. They're the result of a deep frustration born from knowing what really matters.

'In 2019 my stepfather died in our local hospital. This is the same hospital where my sisters were born, which cared for family and friends for years, that trained me (for free!) and gave me my first decently paid job, friends, and huge life lessons. This is where I gave birth to my children and where I said goodbye to people. In other words, this hospital has been one of the most important anchors in my life and I am forever grateful.'

But her stepdad's final months were a struggle, especially for Naomi's mother who is very elderly and unwell herself and didn't understand quite how ill her husband was. A clear diagnosis or prognosis was never forthcoming, they had to fight to get better information at every step.

'Mum later told me that as it finally dawned that her husband was dying, two days before he did, she began crying – and no staff on the ward glanced over or stopped to check she was OK.'

Naomi's stepfather, too, had poor basic support in his final days – no help to ensure he ate, which, as a dementia sufferer who often forgets to eat and drink, was vital.

'At first we were shocked and angry, but my perspective slowly changed as over the days and weeks we realised that these problems were a result of a complex web of issues, "priority" demands and culture.'

Painful as this was, Naomi knew her family's experience was neither shocking nor unusual and the two obvious responses were either to keep quiet and accept the strain on the system, or formally complain. Neither felt right.

Being a pirate, there is always another option: try to change it yourself. She wanted to honour her stepdad's memory and respect all the incredible things the majority of hospital staff did for the community and patients, so over the next few months

Naomi sought out someone within the hospital to discuss what could change and finally got a meeting with a medical director and organisational development manager.

'Cat and I visited, taking Be More Pirate *with us as a peace offering (the book is my 'Dumbo's feather' totem). We had such a lovely welcome and really felt this was an open door. We talked about "re-humanising the system" and about the rules that no longer work. They were really receptive.'*

One aspect that Naomi identified specifically was the dead waiting areas and how they could be used better. There were no quiet rooms or decent outside spaces anywhere to have a private chat or connect with others within the hospital. It created a real feeling of isolation. So, they suggested setting up a 'public living room'; an idea pioneered by a social movement called Camerados. Public living rooms can be set up anywhere by anyone and are simply a makeshift area to meet and talk to people – a social space to help build more connections among strangers, without any particular agenda.

This echoes much of what was said at Macmillan's cancer inequalities event (detailed in chapter seven). Many of the attendees came up with new rules that would increase human connection in clinical settings in order to combat the loneliness that comes with illness. There is great potential for easy interventions that would make life bearable, even enjoyable; an extra couple of chairs here or there, some decoration, and an invitation to talk, yet the more common response to system change is to overcomplicate it. A lot of Naomi's frustration is that the obsession with tool kits and improvement strategy does not actually change much at all.

'We have so many management-related roles, but rarely do any of them facilitate any lasting change or support people, it just creates a pyramid of documents, plans, and meaningless milestones. It's not the workforce's fault but we have gotten into such a mess where everyone just replicates the same structures and approaches at a rapid rate. It's a pandemic of scale and spread. The transactional drowns out the

relational and meaningful – but it doesn't work for complex human issues.'

Naomi's co-pirate, Cat Duncan-Rees, shares this feeling. She previously worked for Stockport Council, but, fed up with being told to work according to the meaningless milestones, she jumped ship to work with the charity Think Local Act Personal and the National Co-production Advisory Group (NCAG), before becoming an independent coproduction advisor and facilitator.

'Local authorities up and down the country have wasted millions over the last few years on project plans and business cases and how they're going to integrate services and work better with communities, and they've got nothing to show for it. Where it has worked, is where people like us have gone in and immersed themselves at any level and asked people – what do you value about living/working here? What don't you like?'

Scaling the wrong things

Every now and again the 'iceberg of illusion' (or success, depending on your perspective) will be re-circulated around the internet. It is a visual demonstration that most of what we need in order to make something or someone successful, lies hidden beneath the water. The outputs we celebrate are just the tip of the iceberg, but because those things feel tangible, we mistakenly make them the focus of our efforts.

It is an image Cat uses to explain why a more human approach to health and social care is a more successful one, and why she takes the time to immerse herself within communities. To create a good service or get the right outcome, first you have to create the right conditions for the people involved. This is not dissimilar to what a Pirate Code achieves, and one of the reasons Cat was drawn to the language and principles of the Golden Age Pirates: they co-created the right conditions for lasting change. Trust, accountability, transparency, good communication, challenge, and an ability to experiment are a few of the conditions she suggests that are key to better outputs, but to get there you have to start by asking better questions: do you feel heard? Who are you connected to?

'We're overcomplicating stuff. Health and care systems have been trying to integrate processes and systems for 20 years, but they haven't really tried to build relationships and trust and networks from the point of view of what matters to people. This is what we desperately need.'

Over the last few years, Cat has experimented with approaches that help people shift from focusing on what the problem is, to understanding why people feel and behave the way they do. It might sound a bit 'fluffy' or even patronising in its simplicity, but asking people to reflect on situations they have experienced themselves and notice the feelings that are invoked, works wonders.

'In order to feel valued, and, understood we all need to have our feelings "heard" and acknowledged. However, the systems and processes we work with don't allow this. They push us towards finding out what the problems are, what the matter is with people, and how we fix them. Rather than talking about the situation itself, inviting people to talk about what contributed to those feelings helps even some of the most "professionalised" professionals to appreciate why the people they are working to support exhibit the behaviours they do.'

Proximity is the problem

So aside from asking different questions, how do you create the right conditions?

Cat's official title is coproduction advisor and coproduction is the approach she uses. It is a simple premise: that to create good, functional services you have to work side by side with the people they are for, in both the design *and* delivery. You don't inform them or consult them (or 'them' them in any way) because only when you work together as equals will you discover the truth about what is really needed. Problems arise and bad rules are created because the people making the most important decisions are too far away from the source to grasp all the detail, or the full implications of their decisions. As the American politician Ayanna Pressley said, *'Those closest to the pain should be closest to the power.'*[17]

Coproduction can feel disorientating at first because it means the professional in the room is no longer necessarily the expert, but one of many people with useful information to share. It does not mean dismissing clinical, or other formal expertise, but examining what kind of information is needed to find a solution, and where that information comes from.

Coproduction upends the usual power dynamics but Cat can churn out example after example explaining why it works. One of the most impactful examples was being a team coach on a Nesta-run 100-day challenge. She worked with everyone involved in different stages of a gastroenterology referral: a nurse, an IBD/gastro consultant, a GP, GP practice manager, an NHS business manager, a patient, and voluntary sector worker. Together, they set themselves the goal of reducing the referral treatment time of people who'd presented to their GP with inflammatory bowel disease from 40 weeks down to eight weeks within 100 days. And they achieved it. Actually, they got it down to 8 weeks and two–three days. But who's counting…

The approach was successful because it got people out of their system silos. Breaking down the silos paved the way for people to make the connections and develop the relationships between the siloed parts of the process.

'My approach is simple. Get people in a room and create a space that makes it safe to talk. I've just adapted that over the years. Inviting people to begin by reflecting and writing down what is important to them in relation to the questions or lines of enquiry being explored.'

Coproduction is only a label, and in some ways risks becoming system fodder, so I'm somewhat loath to use it or define it any further. One of our pirates refuses the word because of this and

17 pressley.house.gov/media/press-releases/rep-pressley-hosts-cbc-delegation-historic-visit-greater-boston#

simply prefers 'creating things together.' It's not a strict method anyway, there are lots of different ways you can do coproduction. Macmillan's sex and cancer workshops are a great example, as are Tammy Watchorn's QUBE teams. Barry Verdin at the Open University coproduced the solutions to his technology overhaul with his colleagues. There have been lots of examples. It's just about how we work together.

The mutiny method that Sam and I use in Be More Pirate workshops (described in chapter five) is essentially a form of coproduction. We ask people to work in small groups of mixed levels and roles. Over the course of the session we ask questions about people's fears and their ambitions, both individually and as a team. We identify the blockers to success and facilitate an environment where everyone is on equal footing and is encouraged to speak the truth. Then we then ask them, together, to write some new rules. The new rules are coproduced and based on an understanding of the real pain points, where the most senior people get a chance to hear from those closest to the problems.

Coproduction as an idea, has been around a while, but is usually pushed aside in favour of consultation or a form of engagement that's more cost-effective and less hassle. The problem is that without it, you may end up with far worse problems later down the line.

Sabotage the system

Another specific technique Cat uses to help people understand how the rules actually work against people rather than protect them, is called 'sabotage the system'. Isaac Samuels, Deputy Chair of the National Co-production Advisory Group, recently used this exercise while talking to a psychiatrist about his own care. He asked her directly:

'…if you were going to build a system, the sole aim of which was to ensure people would have the worst outcome, what would you do? I got a blank face – so I said this is what I would do:

1. *Lock them up and give them very few choices about treatment*
2. *Put them in a hospital in the middle of nowhere*
3. *Make it hard for people to come and visit them*
4. *Make it impossible for professionals that support them to come together to plan their care*
5. *Work in a non-joined-up way*

The penny dropped when the psychiatrist realised that's exactly what we do now.'

This exercise gives you a clear idea of what to stop doing. Interestingly, it really does reflect real-world sabotage strategies, as detailed in the CIA's 1944 'Simple Sabotage Manual'.[18] The booklet describes a set of instructions designed to actively reduce productivity in a workplace. Within it are ideas that constitute a lot of what modern work has now become, such as 'hold conferences when there is more critical work to be done', or 'multiply the procedure and clearances involved in issuing instructions'.

I watched Cat use the Sabotage the System exercise at an NHS Trust event and saw how it adds humour and gravity to a workshop in equal measure. She asked a room of practitioners, in small groups, to write down on one big piece of paper everything they would do to sabotage place-based care. Aside from a few abstract ideas (hold every meeting in French), they came up with things such as 'believing the job can be done brilliantly by never leaving your desk', or 'overworking everyone' and eventually reached the same conclusion: oh shit, we're doing this stuff already.

Rip up the recruitment rule book

Sabotage the system shows what kinds of rules produce poor outcomes; they arise when you start trying to solve a problem from

18 www.cia.gov/news-information/featured-story-archive/2012-featured-story-archive/CleanedUOSSSimpleSabotage_sm.pdf

the point of what the system can currently offer rather than what people need. An area that regularly suffers from this is recruitment. By and large, we're still doing recruitment in the same way we've always done it – with application forms, bullet point packed CVs, and lists of stringent criteria that you must prove you meet in order to interview. Does it get you the right people? More often than not it just gets you the people you'd expect, who have gone to great lengths to shoehorn themselves into the expectations prescribed.

A couple of years ago, Cat was invited to work semi-independently as a community facilitator, coach, and mentor to Winning Hearts and Minds, a programme designed to improve health outcomes within communities in North Manchester.

Why? Dr Cordelle Mbeledogu outlines the scope of the challenge in their interim report:

'More Mancunians are dying early from heart disease than anywhere else in the country, especially in the north of the city. ... Traditional approaches to reducing health inequalities have not had the impact hoped for. Winning Hearts and Minds is "our" response to this challenge. Winning Hearts and Minds has given permission to challenge the norm; begin to rewrite the rules of engagement and try out new ways of working.'

To understand what type of things were having the biggest impact on people's physical and mental health – whether it was crime, lack of transport infrastructure, social isolation, or otherwise – they needed to get into the communities and listen, hard. To do this, the then programme manager Clare Morley, and subsequently Charli Dickinson, endorsed Cat's request to 'break the traditional HR rules' early on. The plan wouldn't work with an identikit group of field workers with all the usual qualifications and experience; she wanted to recruit a team who came from and represented the communities they would work with; who were interested in people and genuinely wanted to understand what was going on.

To try to identify applicants who didn't fit the usual mould but had a real desire to fulfil the brief, the shortlisting criteria were re-written to allow 'anyone who looked remotely interesting on paper' to be shortlisted and a 'pirate score' was added to the criteria for the interactive workshops they ran, which were in place of traditional interviews. Some of the eight fieldworkers they hired wouldn't have made it past the shortlisting round if they'd stuck to the usual recruitment process, yet they have created a team of truly exceptional people, who are now making huge strides on the project.

The northern mutiny

The more Cat and Naomi talked about pirates and how the principles in *Be More Pirate* motivated them to speak up and explain how things could be different, the more they were able to recruit others to the cause. The northern health and social care crew represent the possibility of real opposition to a system that too often malfunctions. It includes some of the most senior leaders within Greater Manchester as well as people with lived experience, and no hierarchy in between. They are a sounding board to each other, a sense check for the decisions that float across their desks and in meetings when they want to say something but feel constrained. They are a constant source of reassurance and inspiration amid rising tensions, budget cuts and some seriously hard times. **Hearing a few encouraging words from your crew on a bad day is the difference between cracking on or giving up.**

To date, Sam and I have been to two events that brought this group together. It was watching them each stand up one by one and articulate a moment in which they realised they *could* challenge the system that first showed me the power of a crew. Their sincerity cut through the stagnation of usual conversations about change, and for the first time in a long time, I thought: here are the leaders we need.

One of the speakers was Jo, a nurse at a hospital in Greater

Manchester; she has been on the front line of care for 23 years but only recently realised the power in her position.

'I've been used to working in a system where I'm told what to do. I do get why we have systems, processes, policies, and rules, but I discovered in the last few years that I have got a voice too and my experience in following the rules can result in ideas for how they can be improved, and that it's OK to speak up.

'I was doing a university module on anatomy and physiology and the tutor said if you haven't got a Twitter account please get one because I'll be posting the course material up there. After following a few anatomy and physiology related accounts, I started browsing and wanted to know if there were any other nurses tweeting… Turns out there's thousands of us, but I realised that what I was actually looking for was pirates, and I've found lots of them.

'I found that speaking up on Twitter and through staff surveys hasn't got me into trouble yet, and, in fact, I've had really positive feedback from some senior leaders at more than one organisation including the one that I work at. I am able to advocate for colleagues who wish to speak up and encourage speaking up in a professional way. If I can give a voice to the front line and be a patient advocate, maybe we can help change the world.'

Another woman who nails down the kind of leadership we need is Claire Tomkinson. She said:

'Is the leader really the person at the top of the organisation with lots of authority? Or is it the person in the middle of the network with lots of people around them who've got their back? What actually achieves things?

'The interesting thing is that our strongest, most effective, and most inspirational leaders often don't consider themselves to be leaders at all, but they are working together, normally outside and beyond their organisations, at the edge of the formal structures of the system to bring about significant change.

'It mainly happens in pubs, coffee shops, corridors, and car parks. Normally after a meeting where they haven't been able to say a word or contribute. Often when they haven't felt safe enough to disagree with

what was being said in the meeting (and realise later that half the room agreed with them and they didn't feel safe enough either) and mainly when they haven't even been invited to the meeting in the first place. We need these real leaders in the system. They are the people that everyone knows, everyone trusts and that can bring people together, not through their authority, but through their vision and their ability to recognise a shared purpose or common cause.'

Sooner or later, the real leaders find each other. They are the substance I was searching for in *Be More Pirate* because they have live battles to fight every day. Often, they sail very close to the wind of their job security, asking the questions no one else will. I have no doubt that the health and social care pirate crew will use their collective power to do something together, in time, but for now the impact seems to be giving each other the courage to start pushing limits in their own corners of the system.

Perhaps the best testament to the impact of this group comes from Isaac Samuels, someone who has had decades in and out of the health and social care system and plenty of bad experiences to report. As a result of being part of this crew, he's started to believe that things could be different.

'Last year, I nearly died because the system wasn't talking to the system. I've been around a long, long, long time and you guys have given me so much hope. Don't forget there are lots of people like me that are at the edge of this place where there's no hope because we don't get to meet and connect with people like you. If we know we have allies, we can do this.'

*

The real bad language

Pirates have long had a reputation for being foul-mouthed (I suppose all the Fuck It Time etc. that we've been encouraging hasn't helped). However, it's not swearing you ought to worry about, it's sentences like this:

'Thinking systemically involves developing parsimonious but insightful ways of understanding the core dynamics of systems.'[19]

Any idea? No, us neither.

But this is pretty standard language in the civil service, in charities, and in academia. The words of the 1%: vague, obstructive, smart-sounding language is not just confusing, it is elitist, and actively gets in the way of doing the work that makes a difference to people. Yet it's also one of the simplest things to change. Language is both the curse and the cure. If you want to try to re-humanise a system, start by looking at the language.

One of the organisations to really focus on this point is CRIN, the children's rights charity. To communicate the problem with language to their audience, they included a jargon buster quiz in their 2018 report, What Lies Beneath, which included questions like this:

Road maps are:

a.   A plan or strategy for achieving a particular goal
b.   The defunct marketing name of Google Street View
c.   An actual map

Road maps are one of the most disliked phrases from a litany of professional jargon smiting our lives. Scour the internet and you'll find long lists of words and phrases that we love to hate. 'Going forward', 'circle back', 'close of play' – inventing vagaries to sub in for what you actually want to say but can't, has become a workplace sport.

It's funny until it becomes insidious. Putting together lots of words that do not produce an immediate association in the mind of the listener or reader results in cognitive overload – that feeling you get when you have to read sentences over and over again before you can understand them. Jargon actively blocks a would-be interested audience from engaging with important

19   p.3, RSA Journal, Issue 3, 2019

topics and is therefore a direct barrier to creating change in the world.

The NGO sector has a particularly complicated relationship with abstract language, so CRIN have included taking a stand against jargon in their code. A preference for words like 'mainstreaming', 'synergy', 'leveraging', and 'catalysing' might sound elegant, but it is highly problematic. Thrown into sentences alongside phrases like road maps, the sense of what is actually being described becomes so ambiguous that people switch off. This is when it becomes dangerous. Sentences that lack clarity also lack gravitas – which is a serious issue when you're talking about human rights. CRIN note that, over time, strong, direct language in relation to human rights has been diminishing in favour of more impotent language:

'In a study of the most commonly used words at the UN Security Council in recent years, examples were ranked from strong to weak, with strong sounding "demands" and "warnings" found to be used less frequently, while the use of weak-sounding "requests" and "urges" for things to be done increased… human rights initiatives have been dotted with pledges and commitments to do a multitude of things followed by a friendly reminder to "honour" them.'

The journalist and environmental activist George Monbiot makes a similar point in relation to how we talk about climate change. If we use language that is neutral or impotent when talking about serious issues, we undermine the cause. Putting it bluntly, he said:

'If we want people to engage with the living world, we should stop using such constipated terms to describe our relationship to it.' [20]

He suggests a range of alternatives to common phrases that might hinder efforts to engage people in climate action:

Biodiversity (too scientific) → wildlife

Climate change (too neutral) → climate breakdown

20   www.monbiot.com/2017/08/11/natural-language

Natural capital (it ain't all there to be bought) → nature/living systems

The Guardian newspaper has followed suit[21] and made six changes to the language their journalists use when talking about the climate, such as moving from global warming to global heating, and climate sceptic to climate denier. Collectively deciding to change language is one of the simplest rebellions you can try.

But what has stopped us from saying what we really mean and inventing new words to use as cover ups? Are we trying to sound like experts? Or is it out of fear of upsetting specific groups, of appearing harsh, unsympathetic, or negative? It requires courage to speak plainly, especially about difficult subjects. But might it be that those you fear upsetting would appreciate the truth the most?

At Macmillan's 'Mind the Gap' event, language barriers were identified as a cause of widening health inequalities. But in the discussion session, it was clear this extended far beyond English being a second language. When participants were asked how they could 'take a risk/rewrite the rules or be more pirate to support people to navigate the system', across all the tables, points were raised about medicalised or indirect language being unhelpful. Comments emerged about 'getting to the point quicker' and the need to decode words like 'stage' and 'grade' at the point of diagnosis.

People also disliked the warlike terminology that refers to cancer as a battle or fight. Built into that kind of lexicon is an implication that survival is a result of personal fortitude and strength of character, which it is not – a point well made by journalist Emily Maitlis[22] on *Newsnight* in relation to Covid-19. Making this link with language denies the disproportionate impact that inequality has on health outcomes, which was precisely what Macmillan's event highlighted.

---

21   www.theguardian.com/environment/2019/oct/16/guardian-language-changes-climate-environment

22   www.youtube.com/watch?v=L6wIcpdJyCI

People living with cancer wanted to be asked how they were – to be addressed as people before becoming just a 'service user' (a widely disliked term). But to really re-humanise the situation, it isn't necessarily about what it said, but who says it. What would happen if the patient were to ask the clinician how they are first and receive an honest answer? This turns the interaction on its head and acknowledges that it may not just be the patient who is de-humanised by the nature of clinical interactions – there is a toll on medical staff too.

Ian Hurst of We Are Hummingbird Health has also experienced issues around language in his work as a mental health first aider.

'We knew that there were people in the music industry that don't relate to mainstream mental health campaigns so we're trying to rip out the rule book. If someone wants to call themselves a fruit loop because that's how they communicate, go for it. It's not "correct" but if communicating prevents suicide then that's what matters.'

So yes, pirates are potty mouths, but humour, swearing, slang, or any other kind of less formal language are sometimes a far better form of communication than precision, so they should not be ruled out just because you're in a professional or formal setting.

Ask the question: **are you communicating as best you can or are you saying it the way you think it should be said?**

Protect what is sacred

Teaching design without practise is like teaching swimming from a book. Sooner or later someone will drown. – Lefteris Heratakis

If there is one realm that further supports how we might re-humanise our systems, it's creativity. Forms of creative expression: drawing, painting, singing, dancing, writing – are ways in which we get out of our head and into our emotions, and on difficult days, where we find relief and solace. The arts are a way of representing and defining ourselves in the world, and of staking a claim on our authenticity before social labels come calling. Creative expression protects the essence of our individual humanity.

The ability to practise art, and for it to be valued within our education system is what this next rebellion is about.

Lefteris Heratakis has been a lecturer in visual communications for over 10 years. After training at UCA Kingston University and the Royal College of Art, he created a successful career in illustration, graphic design, advertising, publishing, and branding. In 2009, he went on to teach at Leeds Beckett University (formerly Leeds Met), and when he first started, he imagined that the university curriculum and set-up would be much like what he'd experienced as a student.

However, the reality was quite different. Virtually none of the values that defined the Art School in the United Kingdom had survived. Instead, he experienced the 'marketisation' of education.

This led him to ask some basic questions:

- Why do students only have 17 hours contact time, when I used to have 40?
- Why are the studios lit so badly and there's no real equipment?
- Why is there no or severely limited drawing practice?
- Why aren't the management asking me how the students are actually doing, if they're worried about recruitment and retention?

He realised the Art School was deteriorating and corporate-style criteria were beginning to govern education. Design students were no longer being taught by practitioners, but by people with PhDs who'd never practised design. Traditional art schools were being absorbed by the university system and judged by the same academic criteria as other subjects with a much bigger focus on research rather than 'doing'.

'Design education should primarily be about doing – drawing, cutting things up, and making. Doing takes you away from just

thinking. If you think too much it becomes mechanical, contrived – and we create a generation of "Mac Monkeys" (as Professor Phil Cleaver puts it). Play is really important. Otherwise it's like trying to learn swimming from a book. You'll drown.'

Inspired by historical movements like the Bauhaus art school and Black Mountain College in North Carolina as examples of free thinking and independent art education, he decided that it wasn't worth trying to tweak or improve from the inside: new structures had to be built from the ground up.

Lefteris has since spent the last six years planning and launching the New Art School. The aim of the school is to foster the talents of the designers and artists of the future by re-energising the original Art & Design school methodology. It began with some field research. Through the Trans-making European project in collaboration with Relais-Culture Europe and Izmir School of Design he was given the chance to go and visit art schools in Poland and Slovenia where they are still practising traditional 'making'-based teaching. He then contacted art and design schools around the world to look at their curriculums to see who was doing interesting things.

However, rather than direct all his attention towards setting up the school itself, Lefteris realised he needed to dedicate equal, if not more, time to publicising what the New Art School stood for. This was the only way he would bring on board world-class practitioners and position the school as a viable alternative.

To date, he has taken two steps towards this. In November 2019, he hosted the first Alicante Design Education Forum in collaboration with Escuela de Arte y Superior de Diseño de Alicante – an event designed specifically to talk about the state of design education and to bring in perspectives from makers: typographers, calligraphers, book binders, people who are practising art – and to highlight why it is valuable.

'It was a miracle it happened. We had no funding, but it shows what teamwork can do. Hundreds of artists, designers, lecturers, and students from Spain and abroad attended, and we had speakers fly in

from the US and UK. There is no other space where this conversation is being had.'

Valencia Design Education Forum 2020 is now in preparation.

The second thing he is doing to talk about his mission is a podcast called *Design Education Talks*, which aims to showcase practise-based work and draw more people into the movement. The survival of the New Art School demands a clear articulation of what it's about and requires a network of supporters.

'The New Art School really came from the discovery that my students were afraid of drawing.

'Because they were afraid of drawing, they were also afraid of looking. Drawing for design is evidence of observation. We were looking at the same thing and seeing things very differently.'

Current curriculums and financial constraints often exclude many creative individuals whose ideas break with convention. The New Art School aims to improve on established routes into the industry by placing skills such as drawing at the centre of its curriculum. It is also not necessarily a binary choice between doing and thinking; it's a way of protecting the process of creative experimentation that comes with simply trying before you fully understand what you're doing. This is what leads to new discoveries.

As Walter Gropius, founder of the Bauhaus movement, said:

'Our guiding principle was that design is neither an intellectual nor a material affair, but simply an integral part of the stuff of life, necessary for everyone in a civilised society.'

*

The means are the ends

As this chapter concludes, there is something important to pin down about what it all adds up to.

Re-humanising our habits, our work, and the bigger systems within which we live is ultimately about *how* we do things – the ways in which we talk, interact, and carry out tasks. Much is said about knowing your why, and it feels very comfortable to focus on the what – the goal or output at the end of the tunnel. Precious little is said about how. But the voyage from why to what makes up the bulk of life. Or as it's captured in one of Myron's Maxims: The process we use to get to the future determines the future that we get.

Until more people take it upon themselves to change their 'how' I believe we will remain stuck in business as usual. It can start with how you word things, dropping the formalities, and adding in humour. It could be changing how you measure things, how you collect information, how you gather people. Extinction Rebellion have paid due attention to this by creating a code of hand gestures and signals to run meetings allowing them to reach consensus more easily, and ensure all voices are heard. Across a movement of hundreds of thousands this is extremely useful for organising people, but it also points towards something bigger: it helps people to understand that they are part of a collective where everyone is of equal value, and losing our sense of this is what has caused the climate crisis.

I've since observed this everywhere. How we do things makes all the difference. For this reason, re-humanising as a concept cannot be quantified easily since it is the sum of all our behaviours across a broad scope of activity and time. You may have noticed that this has been a consistent focus throughout the book, not just this chapter. Pirate Codes and the majority of the new rules that are created as a result of teams being more pirate focus on behaviours: doing less, exploring, challenging, risk-taking, collaborating. It's really not about what to do, but about how to be.

Our 'how' in writing this book, was equally important. Sam and I deliberately wanted to use people's real-life stories to make the idea of changing behaviours not just theoretical, but applied. In my experience of working on social change projects, storytelling as a means to engage people in the work, is vastly underused. Hard facts and data are still favoured as a way to communicate solutions to problems, rather than beginning with an emotional connection, and layering subject-specific knowledge on top of that. It always feels like a missed opportunity.

For this reason, storytelling will be our final *How To*.

Re-humanise the navy: lessons learned

1. Feel your way: in chapter five, we suggested replacing the focus on process with behaviours and mindsets instead. Here we take it a step further and encourage understanding a situation through the lens of our feelings first. Most of the time we ask 'what happened?' rather than 'how did you feel about what happened?' This is not to give precedent to feelings over facts, but to appreciate that how a person feels about something, regardless of what happened, will likely dominate their experience. Sometimes a situation cannot be fixed, it simply has to be aired.

2. Close the gap: the system begins to fail when it is comprised of lots and lots of rules that were created without significant input from the people they will directly affect. This happens all the time across all sectors and while coproduction might seem like an intense and complex solution to implement, there are also lots of other ways that we can start to close the gaps in our understanding of a problem. It can be as simple as spending more time in the communities and neighbourhoods you are intending to serve. Take a day out to go to a conference or a meeting where people are discussing the problem you're hoping to understand. Get as close as you can to the source.

3. Change your language: this is easiest rebellion you can try. If you see too many acronyms, or confusing, inaccessible jargon being used, call it out or refuse to use it. Language is power; it includes and excludes. Take time to think about it and imagine what alternatives you can use, and how it might shape a different story.

4. Get out of your head and into your hands: in our computer-bound world, we spend a lot of time in our heads processing and sorting information. But we are mind, body, and spirit, no? How about bringing some of the body back into work, switching the focus more regularly back to our senses, using our hands so that our heads are free to daydream. Whether it's paint by numbers, Lego, sewing, jigsaws, baking, pottery or the world's best sticker collection, there is deep benefit in spending some time making and letting the problem solving occur in the background.

Chapter Ten

Tell a Damn Good Story

I've been in impossible situations, two hurricanes and quite a few storms; all of them were like being in the centre of chaos where the air becomes white and foamy like a living fog, waves coming from all sides and in impossible trajectories, howling winds with amazing unpredictable gusts and yet, in all this chaos, the sea will give you a sign, a point, a position.

Captain Tonz

What is your all-time favourite story? Have you ever stopped and really thought about why it appeals to you? What about it excites you? What parts do you find yourself retelling?

These days every digital interaction we have with the world is supposed to tell a story. From Instagram to company websites, communication in the digital age has either shifted power out of the hands of traditional gatekeepers or commercialised our most personal narratives, depending on your point of view. Yet the frequency with which we absorb people's stories doesn't make them any less important – storytelling has always been commercialised – it's just that when it's good, you stop noticing.

The fifth R in *Be More Pirate* is to 'Retell – to weaponise the story' and this is no joke. The Golden Age Pirates were the PR masters of their fate; they told tall tales about their own cunning and prowess to ward off attacks and recruit others to the cause. When it comes to enacting change we ought not forget that stories are still one of the most dangerous weapons at our disposal. Any politician with their eyes on the prize knows the need to spin a good yarn, and get their story out there to win hearts and minds.

When I was 23, I had a crash course in political storytelling.

After finishing an undergraduate degree in literature, I made the rash decision to take a postgraduate course in Middle East politics. I had no idea what I was doing but figured it was finally time to move away from fiction and wrap my head around serious matters like international conflict, which I assumed would largely be about government structures, economics, and the UN.

Instead, I discovered that the trajectory of conflict is usually defined by its narratives: nationalist, religious, historical, and personal, and that this extends far beyond government propaganda or stories selected by the media. The way that individual actors join the dots *emotionally* between the events they experience, has an equally profound impact on how a situation plays out. An individual's personal sense of injustice and suffering, or conversely, of power, can trigger uprisings and ceasefires.

Because of this I've since come to believe that there are essentially two kinds of stories: those that we are being told, and the ones we tell ourselves. The latter are more important not only because they're more convincing, but because they are the ones we have control over. Just as Sam reclaimed and retold the story of the Golden Age Pirates, many of us have a need to reclaim our own story and tell it differently. The community have taught me that **weaponising a story is about owning it.**

Too often, we don't believe in the value of our own stories so we hide, bury or brush over the detail. But a good tale doesn't have to be a blockbuster it need only be authentic. You story could contain the one lesson someone else needs to hear. In listening to other people's stories, inch by inch, we start to believe in a new version of what's possible. Stepping temporarily into someone else's dilemma not only encourages empathy, but it helps us to gain confidence in the medium as a means of change. If they are telling their truth, why can't I? Who might I convince?

And let's not also forget that stories exist because they are one of the most enjoyable ways to ingest information. Why not introduce a little bit of the bizarre and improbable into our lives?

So now, by way of inspiration, it's finally time we heard from a more 'traditional' pirate.

Follow the signs

Anthony Brian Cummins, also known as Captain Tonz, was born in a pub in Cambridge, England, in 1944. At the age of 14, he ran away to sea and began sailing around the world with the old Blue Star Line. Arriving in South Africa, naive to the apartheid laws or the context of segregation, he was immediately arrested for talking to the local black population. From there, he was deported to Mozambique; having never even seen a plane before, suddenly he was on one.

At 17, he boarded a Swedish ship where he learned an array of marine skills, eventually catching the attention of a rival ship.

'That ship was owned by a pirate captain. I became a pirate.'

Captain Tonz has smuggled everything, except arms, but was well known (by those in the right circles) for smuggling camels. He's captured ships, stolen ships and been arrested in the US, the UK (many times), Germany, Poland, Russia, Sweden, France, Cambodia, the Philippines, and, of course, South Africa.

In short, he's gone and done all the things people assume pirates do.

He's also a good man with a big heart.

Tony has told us countless fascinating tales of heroic endeavours. From taking on the destructive practice of 'fishing' with dynamite in the Philippines to brokering negotiations with Somali pirates and numerous other surreal encounters which, as he often says, 'No one would believe me if I told them.'

Woven through these stories is always one constant: the sea.

'Water is life, connect to the waters and you are connected to everything. I've been in impossible situations, two hurricanes and quite

172

a few storms; all of them were like being in the centre of chaos where the air becomes white and foamy like a living fog, waves coming from all sides and in impossible trajectories, howling winds with amazing unpredictable gusts and yet, in all this chaos, the sea will give you a sign, a point, a position.'

*

Alone at sea (be it for real or metaphorically speaking), a good pirate must use their senses, as well as their head, to navigate. This does not mean abandoning rationality, it just means listening to your intuition and spotting moments when life is trying to tell you something important. We have heard from the crew that these moments often come in the form of a sign – an indicator of where to go next, recognisable only to you.

During pivotal moments on brand strategy and market positioning, assessing what potential threats lay ahead in deep waters, Tej Samani, founder of the radical education initiative Performance Learning, was reminded through reading *Be More Pirate* why he got into the business in the first place: to give a voice to the ones forgotten and left behind because they, too, felt like misfits and outsiders.

'I thought... this book has come to you for a reason. Are you really being you?'

A sign may come when you're on the edge of a decision, weighing up the pros and cons, tossing and turning at night, analysing the fork in the road. You know in your heart that there is risk associated with staying where you are, and a risk in making a leap into the unknown. Which risk is the risk you need?

After giving a talk last year at the University of Edinburgh Business School, I received the following message from a woman called Jill Kelly.

'I was at your presentation last Monday night and I've been meaning to message you ever since. Loved your honest delivery and the ethos of the book. I had handed in my notice at work and was being persuaded (guilted) into staying. I took a photo of your presentation

graphic (the one at the start that scrolls through words quickly) and it landed on Be More Ruthless, haha! So I've firmly stuck to my plan and new starts in 2020!'

Such messages have become our currency.

One of the very first came from Luana Lewis, an animal welfare officer and mum of two.

'I was on my way to walk my daughter to the dentist, but just after I left home, I realised that I hadn't brought anything to read, and I always bring something for the waiting room. Then out of nowhere as we were walking, I saw this book on the fence just by the common, outside the church. It was staring at me, with those two round, black eyes, I was wearing a pirate t-shirt, and when I picked it up and saw that it said be more pirate – I thought, OK, I understand, this is for me.'

Not long after Luana finished the book, a friend of hers asked if she'd like to come as a guest to any upcoming events at Soho House. He sent over the schedule and lo and behold, Sam was due to give a talk there the following week. Luana came along and told the story of how *Be More Pirate* fast became her bible, giving her the courage to pursue her dreams of starting a business to support and shelter stray animals.

And the stories kept coming.

When TAKK Surf founder Jim Edmondson (from chapter three) returned from holiday having experienced his lightbulb moment to go and create a new type of investment fund, he soon received what seemed like an unmistakable 'go'.

'By complete chance, I actually bumped into Sam at Clapham station, and I had Be More Pirate *in my bag! I told him about the fund and the plan.'*

The signs are the dots you later join to create your story, and all these moments have allowed people to own part of the story of *Be More Pirate.*

Be more Clarence

Undoubtedly, the tales of historical pirates like Anny Bonny, Blackbeard, and Black Sam Bellamy are stirring. You have characters that are both ordinary and extraordinary, flawed but relatable, imbued with enough heroism and naughtiness to make you feel like a badass and a good person in one. But good stories are often repeated versions of the same arc, only with different characters. The reason the book has become a movement is because people have found themselves within *Be More Pirate*. Whether it's Jim seeing surfers as his modern-day pirates or all the countless others who have identified their particular version of the navy – pirates simply represent an idea of challenge that anyone can step into and own.

In chapter six we heard how Alex Dobson brought pirates to his team at Birds Eye. Together they created a host of new rules that enabled them to do more by doing less. But it didn't end there. They not only rewrote the rules of their culture, they rediscovered their legacy. He decided to use his 'Fuck It Time' to dive back into the company history and understand exactly how frozen food came to be. What he found was that the warm and fuzzy Captain Birds Eye we love and trust was definitely a pirate.

The company's real founder, Clarence Birdseye, was not actually a sea captain (the advertising mascot didn't arrive until 1967), but he was a rather unusual character. Born in New York in 1886 into a family of nine children, from a very early age he became obsessed with natural sciences. So much so that by the age of 11 he'd taught himself taxidermy and began offering courses on the subject to his school peers.

Clarence went on to excel in science; after graduation, he became a naturalist and was promptly employed by the United States Agriculture department. It was during an assignment in Canada that he became interested in methods for freezing food. He learned from the Inuit communities how to ice fish under thick ice and noticed how quicker freezing preserved the freshness of the fish and that the quality was much higher than conventional frozen foods at the time.

He went on to found Birdseye Seafoods Inc, introducing this method, but by 1924 his company went bankrupt due to lack of consumer interest. However, Clarence did not give up. He went back and refined the method, using new machinery and a new company name: General Seafood Corporation. In 1927, he extended the novel freezing methods to meat, poultry, fruit, and veg and by 1929 he sold the company and its patents for $22 million.

And that's cutting the story short. In essence, Clarence Birdseye was experimental, he trusted his instincts and found inspiration in unusual places. The lesson? Be brave, be curious, learn from failure. Following Alex's research, the team at Birds Eye realised they didn't really need to be more pirate at all, they just needed to be more Clarence. The story they needed was there all along.

Failure makes the story

As discussed in chapter six, the 'fail fast, fail often' mantra might make you roll your eyes when it's trotted out at work, but, in the context of producing a good story, failure, and even our *failings*, really are an asset. You can't have a story that is flat. There has to be a dip somewhere. No one watches a film or reads a book and skips to the moment of glory at the end. We're interested in the journey – the less predictable the better. Would Clarence Birdseye's success feel quite so 'wow' if he hadn't first gone bankrupt? People relate to failure, so if any part of your work involves telling your story, the experience of failing is part of your value proposition. You're here to live a rich life, not a smooth one. That's part and parcel of being pirate, and worth remembering when the dips are draining, demoralising or even devastating… it is all part of a longer story arc. If you want to really weaponise your story, you need some failure in your life.

And one day, your current failure might enable someone else to believe that it does get better. Your story, told well, could contain the sign someone else really needs to change the course of their life. As Brené Brown says in her talk for 99U It Isn't the Critic That Counts: *I know it sounds cheesy and clichéd to think a quote can change your life, but sometimes when you hear something, and you need to hear it and you're ready to hear it, something shifts inside of you.*

Stories can be informative, but their grander function is to make us feel something. Why on earth do we re-read books or re-watch films when we know the ending? We're looking for the feeling, not the information. Which means that a story doesn't actually have to convey anything new or novel, it can be about *how* you tell it. Told well, the story has stand-alone impact – it is an end in itself.

What is our new story?

In the wake of the 2019 UK General Election, and in response to the feeling of 'OK what now?' the journalist and climate activist George Monbiot tweeted this:

*'We work together to craft the **story** of change: the great missing element in our politics. This is not the same as policies or principles or values…The story is the vehicle that carries them.'*

The real story that needs crafting isn't our individual one of failure or success as we leap from job to relationship, across borders and back again. It's about who we are all together. We can no longer ignore the fact that our entire story, as humankind, must change.

That story needs some magic; some Harry Potter meets Treasure Island to get us off our arses and get some skin in the game. We keep experiencing what feels like seismic shifts in how we exist together and yet we haven't found a story to carry us into the future safely. The story of what global citizenship means is ripe for a rebrand and I don't think we can afford to leave our imagination behind. We can't keep using words that don't excite; we can't keep playing into tired, diminutive 'us vs them' narratives, ignoring that all of us are just trying to make sense of what's happening, without anyone really having a total monopoly on truth. We are all funny and flawed and fallible, but can we make proper space for each other? Can we scrape some of the nuance off the floor, and piece together something that inspires us enough to stop accepting that what is, is the only way it can be?

In the absence of this new story, and in the absence of decent leadership, the spirit of pirates feels like one we need, where all people don't just 'matter' passively, but are involved, actively, in shaping the future – without needing permission. Then, I hope that more pirate leaders emerge and the story starts to take clearer shape, with the necessary grit, guts, and a dash of swashbuckling glamour.

So we will leave you with this: a final story you are unlikely to forget, from Captain Tonz.

'An example of pure connection with the sea occurred one night when I was off the coast of Algeria. Alone on the bridge, I had become angry at the constant bad wave formation I was having to deal with (pirates often have to sail strange, difficult routes). I became so angry I opened the window and shouted at the sea… I will always remember my words, "What the fuck are you doing to me? Why are you giving me this constant fucking hard time, you can fuck off!"

'I felt much better after that and rolled up a smoke to calm me down, but before lighting it something very strange happened. The sea suddenly became impossibly flat calm, I had never seen such a thing. In almost an instant from being a constant wave to a flat calm as flat as oil. The event woke the crew who were used to sleeping with the banging of the constant wave, I was asked what happened, and I said a very worried "I don't know" but I knew it would never happen again.

'Connecting to the sea connects you to life. Connecting with the sea has few requirements, no mathematics, physics or Oms. All you need is empathy and love.

'Then who knows, if you do connect and make a wish, you may even become a pirate, but in any case, you will be changed.'

Tell your story: lessons learned

1. Be your own Clarence: How well do you know your own story? People connect with what's personal so it's worth spending some time mapping out the moments in your life that you really connect with. Why were they meaningful or pivotal? How do they ladder up to what you're doing now? What moment really informed your current values? Helping people to understand why you do what you do through a series of short anecdotes is a powerful weapon to have up your sleeve.

2. Use your failures: The dip in your story, whether it's an individual one or the company story, might be the most compelling part of all. Don't bury or leave it out, the insights are equally valuable. Hearing the dip in your story could pull someone else out of theirs.

3. The story of us all: We need a new story that feels as compelling as it is inclusive. How can you find the pirate story in the now moment? We all have examples of the stories we find most moving. How do we draw out the essential elements and hook it onto the story we're trying to build: a story that stirs us to act?

Chapter Eleven

What Next?

What the stories in the book demonstrate to me is an opportunity for a new kind of protest, one where we are not simply standing at the gates throwing stones at the system from outside, but inside, unpicking it through consistent rule-breaking.

This is a different kind of work. It requires you to find the courage to stand up and challenge in situations when quite the opposite is expected of you. When there is enormous pressure to conform and agree. In those moments you will not be carried by the sound of a crowd, or necessarily feel like you are doing the right thing. People may try to talk you down, tell you that things cannot change and make you feel stupid for believing they even should. Or perhaps worse, you will face a wall of apathy.

However, now is the time to confront the passivity of doing good in the usual ways. To stop pretending that giving to charities or signing petitions is enough. Charity, petitions, and protests are not solutions, they are symptoms that the system is faulty to begin with. We should be aiming to dismantle it and build something better. The actions required to do that are wide ranging, and sometimes more subtle than what we would usually associate with becoming part of a social movement. But a social movement is what this is.

It was important to me that this book did not simply showcase game-changing campaigns, as many books about activism do, but highlight instead day-to-day efforts to break rules, where it feels less sexy. This is needed to move activism away from something only certain types of people do, towards being a vital part of citizenship. Being more pirate is for everyone, everywhere: it doesn't matter how diverse and different our interests and situations are, what our particular fears or barriers are, there is always something we can do, and there is a community waiting to salute your efforts.

And a time is coming, whether we like it or not, where such significant change is likely that we won't have a choice but to unravel the old and build anew. The climate and ecological crisis is no longer a story that can be read as a single issue or one option in an array of causes to support. Climate is the setting within which all other issues – poverty, racism, healthcare, and democracy – will play out. It will touch everything. We are going to have to adapt, materially and psychologically, to different ways of existing together. In weathering the storm, being a pirate is the armour you may need.

Sam and I will strive to provide a platform for aspiring pirates; we will create more resources to support creative rule-breaking and continue to gather the community together so that ideas can be sourced and shared. But my ambitions lay beyond this. I want to see many more new crews forming outside of formal structures, so that while the old models fall, new ones are already emerging. There is plenty of evidence that it is possible and desirable to change the current social contract. For too long we have been putting economic value in the wrong places. The climate crisis is likely to cut through our current structures like a knife to butter, and we better be ready with something else.

Pirates, lead the way.

The Pirate List 2.0

An update on Sam's original list. Detailed below are all the organisations and individuals mentioned throughout this book. With love and deep gratitude to them all.

Natalie Clarkson, the girl who took on the Home Office, find her on
Twitter: @NatalieJosh

Julie Reid, a writer exploring climate solutions, head of content at planetSHINE
planetshine.com

Jim Edmondson, entrepreneur and technologist, founder of TAKK Cap and TAKK Surf
takkcap.co.uk
takk.surf

Traidcraft, the original fair trade pioneers in the UK
www.traidcraft.co.uk

Veronica Yates, Director of the Child Rights International Network (CRIN), a creative think tank that produces new perspectives on human rights issues. Co-founder of the Rights Studio, an arts-driven social enterprise in Berlin.
home.crin.org

Nicola Burnside, Head Of Marketing at Mercedes-Benz Vans UK

Robbie Greatrex, Creative Director and Founder of Mere Mortals
www.meremortalslondon.com

Professor Andrew Sharman, international leadership consultant, President of the *Institution of Occupational Safety & Health* ('IOSH') and Chairman of the Board of the *Institute of Leadership & Management.*
fromaccidentstozero.com/andrew-sharman

Mr and Mrs Smith, global travel club for the adventurous hotel lover
www.mrandmrssmith.com

Helen Timbrell, consultant, researcher and coach in people and organisational development

Crystal Eisinger, Head of Brand and Editorial, Google UK and co-host of the Greater than 11% podcast
Twitter: @CrystalEisinger,
IG: @crystal_maze

Isaac Samuels, Deputy Chair of the National Co-production Advisory Group

Alex Dobson, senior creative strategist and brand innovator

Matthew Cook, helps people realise their potential at Gravity Road and is the creator of 'a beautiful something'
IG: @abeautifulsomething

Barry Verdin, business change specialist at the Open University
Twitter: @Barry_Verdin

Tej Samani, founder of Performance Learning
myperformancelearning.com
IG: @tejsamani

Oksana Pyzik, Senior Teaching Fellow and Global Engagement
Lead at UCL School of Pharmacy, Founder of UCL Fight the
Fakes, Global Health Advisor & Board Trustee Commonwealth
Pharmacists Association
Twitter: @OksanaPyzikUCL, @UCLFightsFakes
         @CW_pharmacists

Sarah Davis, artist and member of Macmillan's London Cancer
Community
linktr.ee/sarahdavisartist

Lourdes Colclough, London Engagement Manager at
Macmillan

Emma Quintal, London Engagement Lead at Macmillan
Twitter: @EmmaQuintal

Nia Lewis, Learning Architect and **Fred Heidt**, Principal at
Youth Inc
www.youthinc.org.au

Josh Moorhouse, storyteller and social innovator
Twitter: @joshmlife

Nick Martlew, Deputy Executive Director at Digital Action
Twitter: @SadMartlew

Dr Tammy Watchorn, change agent, coach, educator, facilitator
tammywatchorn.com

Sarah Shead, producer and founder of Spin Arts, and Captain of the Artistic Mutiny
www.facebook.com/groups/artisticmutinyuk
www.spin-arts.com

Franziska Elmer, coral reef scientist and instigator of Climate Pirates
franziskaelmer.weebly.com
IG: @climate_pirate
@shooting_seastar

Deana Wildgoose and **Ian Wilson**, co-founders of TH!NK FC and Coalville C.A.N
thinkfc.org.uk

James Berg, founder of Picaroons the social media marketing crew, built on pirate principles
www.picaroons.co.uk

Ian Hurst, founder of We Are Hummingbird Health
www.wearehummingbird.com/wahbh-who-are-we
IG: @wearehummingbird
Facebook: @wearehummingbirds

Kath Smythe, Transformation Strategic Lead at Manchester City Council
Twitter: @KathSmythe

Cat Duncan-Rees, coproduction advisor and facilitator, founder of Curators of Change
Twitter: @CatDRees

Naomi Davies, Programme Manager at Nesta and longtime health and care mischief-maker
Twitter: @naomiworldz

Claire Tomkinson, Strategic Lead for Collaboration at Macc
Twitter: @what_claire_did

Lefteris Heratakis, designer, lecturer, podcaster and founder of
the New Art School
about.me/heretakis
newartschool.education

Luana Lewis, animal welfare
IG: @pawsandpirates
pawsandpirates.com

Anthony Cummins, the pirate
captaintonz.com

Acknowledgments

Beyond the incredible pirates who live in the pages of the book, there are many more people who have made Be More Pirate what it is.

First of all to Crystal Mahey-Morgan, Jason Morgan, and the team at OWN IT!, our publishers, who brought this book to life. Their support, vision, and dedication turned everything around in a wildly ambitious timeframe. We cannot thank them enough for sticking with us.

Further thanks must go to Helen Coyle for some early, and much appreciated, editorial support, to Salena Godden and Sophia Thakur whose poetry uplift the text, and to the fantastic creatives who created and developed the Be More Pirate brand: Joe Kibria, Harry Harrison, Bryn Walbrook, Lloyd Scott, Inga Spitzer, Nick Sammons, and Tom Baker.

Sam

I would like to thank some of the wonderful people who got behind the Be More Pirate adventure from the very beginning and opened up the space that allowed the talk and the workshop to emerge. I didn't then know how important a part of the journey that would be. I'm so grateful for the following people who have pushed me and made time to give intelligent, thoughtful feedback as Be More Pirate evolved: David Over, Mathias Lord, Nick Gold, Crystal Eisinger, Paul Hewitt, Philip Miles (and a dozen more Googlers), Christopher Kingsman, Andrew Sharman and Stuart Hughes, Michelle Minnikin, Tom Goodwin, Elly Tomlins, Nick Hampton, Laura Hagan, and Helen Boardman, Jude Pullen, Edward Pinchard, Alastair Thomann, Stuart Almond, John

Showalter and Sarah Logan, Max Alexander, Polly Cochrane and Alex Lewis, Sherilyn Shackell and the Marketing Academy crew.

And, most importantly, my brilliant mentor Liam Black and dear friends Adam and Charlotte Day-Lewin who have helped me to weather the stormiest of seas.

Alex

The first thanks go to all the pirates who make up this movement – the book belongs to you. I'd like to express particular gratitude to the following people who have in different ways, been a great support to me personally in creating the community, through sharing their platform, spreading the message, inspiring me and continually proving how meaningful this all is:

Clare Gage, Paul Stepczak, Colin Newlyn, Scott Seivwright and Sathpal Singh, Tom McCallum, Felicity Healey-Benson, Nick Heard, John Huigen, Gemma Hallett, Chris Edwards, Louize Clarke, Rajwinder Cheema, Julia Kitteringham, Mark Newey, Ruth Leonard and Jo Gibney, Clenton Farquharson MBE, Sally Percival, Olly Benson, Paul Hine, Mark Kingston, Jackie Le-Fèvre, Gilly Lee, Peta Stross, Nardia Joy Lloyd-Ashton, Jo Williamson, Ruth Bromley, Rob Ward, Lucy Paine, Anna Hyde, Ben Reynolds and Lucy Bedall, Galahad Clark, Cath Sloan, Geraldine Hills, Natasha Shafi, and Darko Buldioski.

Additional thanks go to Professor Phil Cleaver for arriving at the opportune moment and being the sign I needed to start writing this book. And, to Andrew James for his longstanding belief in me as a writer without which I'd be somewhere else entirely.

Finally, I'd like to thank my best friends Marina Boshnakova, Hero Mackenzie, and Oksana Pyzik who both challenge and champion me; my parents Katie and Steve for unwavering love and support, and for always offering one part adventure, and one part stability; and my brother George and sister Rosie, you are both bonkers and brilliant, and no one will ever make me laugh more than you two.

Biographies

Sam Conniff is a lifelong advocate of business as unusual, operating at the intersection of brands, policy, and social innovation to create positive change in the world. He is co-founder of award-winning youth marketing agency Livity, Don't Panic, Live Magazine, Dubplate Drama and Digify Africa, and author of the international bestseller *Be More Pirate or How to Take on the World and Win*. As a consultant, he advises brands such as Tate & Lyle and Rolex on sustainability, accountability, and 'Professional Rule Breaking'.

Alex Barker leads the Be More Pirate community and wears many hats as a freelance writer, facilitator, and speaker. Before teaming up with Sam to develop Be More Pirate from a book into a movement, she was communications manager at the RSA (Royal Society of Arts). Alex has also worked freelance for author and adventurer Alastair Humphreys, and with writer and activist Onjali Q. Rauf on domestic violence issues.

Captain's Log

Captain's Log

Captain's Log

Captain's Log

Captain's Log

Captain's Log

Captain's Log

Captain's Log

Captain's Log

Captain's Log

ABOUT OWN IT!

OWN IT! is a storytelling lifestyle brand, sharing stories across books, music, art and film. At the heart of everything we do is a desire to share, empower, celebrate and inspire. Whether it's through multi-media digital books, print books, music or film, OWN IT! releases original and authentic stories told in creative new ways.

WWW.OWNIT.LONDON